Contents

Foreword

Jacob Ecclestone

OF ALL the great issues which perplex and divide our society —
unemployment, nuclear weapons, civil liberties and so on — none, I
believe, is more dangerous than racism. What makes racism unlike
all other political problems is that it is the product of the irrational
and is, therefore, not easily dealt with by reasoned discourse.
Unlike other problems, too, we are all in varying degrees victims
of the poison of racial prejudice. Racism is part of the fabric of our
history, woven into our Imperial past, and although we have shed
our colonies — or most of them — we have not succeeded in
shedding the ideologies and attitudes which underpinned our military and economic subjugation of other races and cultures.

But we must continue to make the effort. We have to recognise
— whether we like it or not — that Britain is a multi-racial society
and will remain so. There can be no going back. Until we accept,
indeed positively welcome and take pride in, the social and cultural
richness of our diversity, then we remain set on a course of permanent conflict.

Southall...Bristol...Brixton...Toxteth...Moss Side were the
entirely predictable — and predicted — consequences of our failure
to purge ourselves of feelings of racial superiority.

Those of us who have never had to endure the pain, the daily
round of indignities and discrimination, should feel remorse that we
have not done more to resist the racism that is all around us. We
should feel some humility, too, at the tolerance shown by black
people in our community in the face of their oppression.

More than anything, however, we should feel an angry deter-
mination to put an end to the evil of racism. By remaining silent,
whether singly in casual conversation, or collectively when faced
with institutional racism, we condone something which is an affront
to civilised standards of behaviour and our democracy.

This book, drawing together a variety of points of view and
dealing with various aspects of racism in the newspaper and broad-

---

* *Jacob Ecclestone is Deputy General Secretary of the National Union of
Journalists.*

casting industries, will, I hope, help to make us think more clearly and deeply about our responsibilities as people who are in the business of communicating ideas.

I am repeatedly struck — and saddened — by the hostile resistance of journalists to any serious scrutiny of their role in society. Journalists spend their working lives observing, analysing and commenting on what other people do; they are absurdly unwilling to consider and question their own attitudes and methods of work.

It is crucial, I think, to the future of our society that we, who are responsible for the dissemination of ideas, are made to stop and think about how — mostly unconsciously — we are contributing to and reinforcing racial stereotypes and prejudices.

If the articles which follow have the effect of making even one journalist stop to assess the effect of what he or she is writing or saying, then the effort will have been worthwhile.

Introduction

CARM, race and the media: the story so far

Geoffrey Sheridan

How much should be read into a headline? On June 15, 1982, when 'Our Boys' had re-conquered the Falklands, page one of the London *Standard* trailed: 'The first man in Stanley'. Since the man was their own reporter, we should perhaps grin and mark it down to the promotion department. Yet the evocation of all those yarns about the 'discovery' of America, Africa, and much of the rest of the globe by intrepid Europeans isn't really funny – or, in the case of the *Standard*, likely to have been accidental.

The Falklands war brought to the fore a putrid concoction of jingoism and racism, to the extent that *Private Eye*'s spoof front page of the *Sun*, with the cry to 'Kill all Argies', needed to be looked at twice to be sure that it was a send up. Britain's strength as a global power peaked in 1850, but its heritage is still very much with us today, marking all major political parties, institutions, and classes of British society.

It was another front-page story which gave rise to the Campaign Against Racism in the Media. On May 4, 1976, the *Sun*'s banner headline announced: 'Scandal of £600-a-week immigrants'. The page was adorned with a photograph of a row of Asian refugees looking anxious and angry. They had been posed holding up their British passports, which in a different time and place would have been the Yellow Star of David.

There was nothing ambiguous about the article, which concerned two Asian families expelled from Malawi, less their possessions. On their arrival in Britain, the local authority had placed them temporarily in a hotel, hence the £600 cost. On May 5, the *Daily Mail* hit on another angle: 'We want more money, say the

* *Geoffrey Sheridan was secretary of CARM between 1976-78 and currently works for New Socialist. He is a member of the national committee of the Campaign for Press and Broadcasting Freedom.*

£600-a-week Asians'. This was their reply to the question: 'Do you need more money?' — hardly a surprising response when both were large families being paid £46 a week by social security. Behind the story was British imperial globe-trotting. Asians had originally been brought to East Africa as indentured labour to build the railways, and then left to their own devices. But that wasn't of interest to the *Sun* or the *Mail*. The 'scandal' broke at a time of increasing activity by the fascist National Front, when physical attacks on blacks in Britain were fast becoming a daily occurrence. Anti-racists in the National Union of Journalists considered that Fleet Street's front pages were fuelling this violence. On July 15, 1976, some 60 NUJ members came together to launch CARM.

From its inception, the campaign took the view that countering mass media racism could not be effectively undertaken solely from within. There needed to be a pincer movement, bringing pressure to bear from those on the receiving end of racist bias on those responsible for producing it; while union policies and activities could be hammered into shape.

The early days

CARM's initial role was that of midwife, holding meetings at which blacks met journalists. Such encounters proved constructive, if sometimes — as in the case of the *Tottenham Weekly Herald* in the early days of the campaign — loud and angry. If some journalists did not hide their bigotry, many were concerned to say that while their heart was in the right place, their mind had to be tuned to 'neutrality', 'impartiality', and other such nostrums instilled by their training and required by their editor. We asked if they really thought they should be neutral between racism and anti-racism. And the explicit and covert messages of articles and radio and TV programmes were spelled out to show that too often they reinforced racist beliefs in a deeply racist society.

An instrument quickly grasped within the NUJ was the union's Code of Conduct, at the time a rarely mentioned feature of the union's rules, although every applicant for membership agrees to abide by it. A clause forbids the encouragement of discrimination on the grounds of race or colour. Early complaints under the code met with no success; but at last it was on the map, and the code has come to be seen as a major statement on press freedom, the battle for which has come to the fore within the labour movement.

Exposing media racism and explaining how it could be countered — in a phrase, producing propaganda — was inherent in

3

*How the press
incites racism:
1976 – the 'Asians' at the
centre of the story are not even quoted;
1982 – press uncritically lap up
police attack on 'black crime'.*

CARM's foundation, and it has since become our principal activity.

The campaign's first pamphlet, *In Black and White: Racist Reporting and How To Fight It*, sold out 2,500 copies within months of its printing in 1977. That dealt exclusively with the press. *It Ain't Half Racist, Mum*, the campaign's TV exposé of television's own racism, was made as an 'Open Door' programme and was seen by an estimated third of a million viewers when it was first shown on

BBC-2 shortly before the May 1979 General Election. We received over 800 letters from viewers, and the film continues to be widely shown at meetings and in schools.

BBC picketed

The Open Door programme was very nearly not transmitted at its scheduled time, BBC management being sensitive to the impending election. The reason was easy to fathom. The Anti Nazi League had succeeded in labelling the National Front as Nazi in the minds of millions, and the NF's vote was to collapse in the election. Militant black groups were asserting their rights and defending lives and property in their communities. Racism and fascism became distinctly unfashionable within the labour movement, which is a long way from implementing black rights, but it was an important start.

The National Front secured a five-minute party political broadcast during the election campaign, and there were pickets outside ten TV studios – jointly called by the ANL and CARM – to condemn it.

Every union in print and broadcasting has established formal policies to oppose racism, and there has now been valuable backing for black media workers by the National Union of Journalists and the Association of Cinematograph, Television, and allied Technicians (ACTT). The industry was one of the first to see the formation of a black group to advance their interests. The Black Media Workers Association, set up in 1980, has grown in numbers and influence, and it has modified CARM's role. So, too, has the Campaign for Press and Broadcasting Freedom, formed in 1979, and now supported by the TUC and over 20 trade unions.

In short, there is now a broad front campaign against the welter of bias heaped on working people by the mass media, and an organised group of black media workers to challenge racism within the industry, especially as it affects the employment of blacks in the various jobs which lie behind its productions.

For a black view of Britain to be effectively communicated to white Britons, such employment is vital. For blacks themselves, the development of their own press and access to broadcasting immeasurably aids the self-confidence and self-organisation required to assert black rights.

CARM's membership has been predominantly white. Do we still have a role to play? In part, the answer lies in this pamphlet. Readers can judge for themselves the progress that has been made, and how much yet remains to be challenged.

Black autonomy and the BBC

Alex Pascall interviewed

Alex Pascall has been presenter of Black Londoners on BBC Radio London since 1974. In late 1981 he was involved in a series of struggles with BBC management over the programme's form and funding. This account is based on an interview with Phil Cohen.

Let's take the name *Black Londoners* – the community is such a wide one that you must be careful of the name you put on a programme. I don't think the authorities realised that the name *Black Londoners* would have lasted, otherwise they might not have allowed it. Because every time I would listen to them saying 'If only, Alex, we could find a different name for the programme, because the white community don't like it really'.

But it has meant that the programme has moulded black people from all different parts of the world – because we never knew each other in the Caribbean; island didn't know island, country didn't know country. Now the word black is the norm. It's still not the accepted norm in the mind of the constructors and holders of the media. They don't really like it.

We started off with little money – we were told we could have the airspace but there was no budget, so for the first six months I didn't get paid. When a new manager, Alan Holden, came in he said he would try and find money because he thought it would mush-room. At that time the programme *Reggae Time* was the thing on Sundays. When I came on the station, the programme was put under 'Education', and the apparatchiks were saying 'make sure this programme will be something we'll be proud of and High Commissioners will like to go to it'. Stuff the High Commissioners – left to them the programme would still be in limbo. Now the High Commissioners are on the programme but they have to be with it because the tide of change in Britain makes no doubt about that.

I can never forget the first day the programme went out – people were expecting the messiah to come. I couldn't tell you what it ould be like because I went into the studio three days before, there was no training given, I was told this is a knob there, if you want to make contact with us through the glass touch that. But I wasn't frightened. I'd come from showbusiness where I'd worked as a comedian, as a singer, so really I had to adapt from stage to radio. I was more inclined to be funny than serious but they were willing to take a programme. I wonder now whether the Beeb themselves expected it to last, I think they did not.

'Give up' I was told

Originally there was just me involved plus three young women who helped me in the first few programmes and then said they couldn't go on, they wanted to be paid. From 1974 to 1978 I was alone. From 78 to 79 someone from Bush House was seconded to the programme in a secretarial position to help, Carmen Gordon. Then she became pregnant and went to have her baby. Some people told me to give it up because of the pay. After a year they started giving me £15 a programme – OK it might be said local radio doesn't have much money. The CRE gave £200 at the inception for expenses and were then asked for more. So up to 1978 when the CRE gave £3000 I was getting £13 a week and Radio London were paying me £24 so in all I was getting about £40 to do that whole once-a-week programme on a Friday night. And that was a tough hard slog of one and a half hours. It was really cheap labour. People told me that, but I had to prove the point that I could do the job. My wide experience prevented them attacking me as they might attack anybody else.

Just a year before Alan Holden arrived I had a feeling the station had a problem and might close because the audience figures were low. Alan saw the potential of *Black Londoners* and he sent me on a tour of the Caribbean and in six weeks I covered eight islands. I came back and then in May 1978 the programme went from weekly to daily. When I went to FESTAC 77 in Nigeria that was a big thing for me. I was the only person here to come back with material, although the BBC sent many people from different areas and they spent money I didn't have. I never realised what an experience it would be for those listening – they were living what I actually lived.

One hour per day cannot be enough. You must put bits of us into the general programmes and that never happens. There were two cases of us giving things to Radio 1 having offered them to Radio London and being turned down. But when Radio 1 put it out they copied it and put it out on Radio London.

They wanted to give me a secretary. After Carmen went Juliet Alexander came. I still kept asking for a secretary and they eventually said they would ask Manpower Services. Juliet and I interviewed about 12 trainees and picked Eunice Jackson. After six months they decided she must go and said take another one, I said that she needed more experience with us. I realised the game which was never to give us a secretary. She stayed for another six months. What they have been doing is putting Malcolm Laycock, he is now the producer, as a buffer plate between management and us. It amounts to racism, industrial racism, it is actually saying your people are not equivalent to our people. It's putting you in a little corner like it's a political slot we have to maintain to keep the minorities quiet. I mean there was a time when they wanted to do a programme on Brixton and they came to ask me to find them two 'muggers'. There was a piece in *The Guardian* about a guy who put a microphone on his body and went down to Brixton to get mugged. He didn't get mugged and I was sorry he didn't get mugged.

Blacks in a corner

There were times, too, when I was broadcasting things about the Notting Hill carnival and when I listened to the news it was contrary. I would be at carnival and a guy comes from nowhere and says 'do a bit about the police'. Look at the Jewish programme, Michael presents and produces it. Country and Western produced and presented by... why is it the black and Asian programmes that they can't allow this? What are they frightened of? A producer has certain perks and rights and it means you're getting into the high structure of the Beeb — they don't want that.

I have never shouted 'racist' but there are racist behaviours here, no one could deny that. It is a very institutionalised form of racism. To show how it goes deeper, when Keith went on holiday, he left Malcolm in charge; when Malcolm went on holiday he left a freelance who is junior to me by far in charge. So everyone from a white point of view was always in charge of the education room where I work. They are trying to harass me to leave so they could take over the structure but the community is taking them on. The CRE has shown we have about 45,000 listeners a day. If I walked out and quit, the station would be broken up in hours, there is no police force that could stop it. There is an action committee taking the fight over and getting support from masses of white people. Sacking me will not solve it, there will be 10 more to come.

I think the people in power in the BBC are very, very scared of

Susie Martin

Alex Pascall and assistants planning another Black Londoners *show in the Radio London studio.*

black people and they are very distant as to how the masses of people are thinking. There are more youth studying journalism than anything else and when they come out, the colleges call me and ask if the students can spend a day with me. You need a workshop.

People listen in partly because they don't know what Alex will come up with each day. I do work differently. The media generally is too slick; everything is too sifted and I don't think the BBC want that change. I have been given a free hand and now they want to take the free hand away. So I couldn't stay because that is what has made the programme. This is a heavy piece of weight to take on, I care about it. It must be produced by a black person who understands the structure, not a BBC person. The people I have been serving understand my problems and they are happy I didn't remain inside and pretend all was well. It has made me a stronger person in the community.

The Black Londoners Action Committee made the following statement during the programme crisis of late 1981 — reprinted from Caribbean Times.

'A battle we cannot afford to lose'

Our relation to the media as Black people is often presented from the point of view of those who are mere puppets and subjected to the barbarity of a racist European culture.

The outcome is that we are rarely given a chance to reflect on that area of the media (namely the radio), within which we have gained a foothold.

The political tension of the early 70's threw up a political community which sought outlets for its frustrations. The BBC gathered up a strand of this energy and utilised it under the heading of the 'access' programme.

The ideas behind access programmes were clearly motivated by some misinformed notion of what constituted good race relations, to quote the 1978 Home Office Report on Broadcasting: 'Each station should have a general duty to inform entertain and educate, but that each should have a special obligation to celebrate the particular quality of life in its locality.

'...for example a local radio station can reflect the differing culture of the ethnic minorities and respond to their special needs'.

Black life is to be used as a bait to lure an audience.

The programme was in fact intended for the White liberal element who sponsor what passes for black culture, black programmes made for White people from a White point of view, as part of the contribution to the anti-racist struggle.

Hence they expect us to be in a state of high exultation, and gracefully receive the crumbs from the Masters table.

Access then was seen as a way in which people could change how they were publicly regarded. But this implies that the media do not expect us to treat White people as unimportant in the making of our programmes.

Yet it is this same treatment that we receive at the hands of the media daily, but somehow we are able to understand it, and ask for no special dispensation!!!

Our programmes have no input into the mainstream programmes. It's only when a problem arises (e.g. the summer uprising) that black staff are allowed to make a contribution to the mainstream, by articulating a black point of view. On such occasions our people are thrust to the forefront of news reporting and used as a front to gain access to the black community.

We are not supposed to have views on subjects such as housing or the education system, or deemed competent to carry out interviews on such topics.

Programmes such as Black Londoners, which command a 59 per cent listenership among London's Afro-Carib community and go out five days a week, like 'Sanghan' in Leicestershire, have become a national and international prominence, are deserving of a proper budget, facilities, and editorial control.

The staff who produce these programmes have to work full time to gather the material to do what is in fact a fully professional job.

The training acquired has been solely 'on the job', thus black reporters have not been through a career structure.

The situation Black Londoners finds itself in is very much a reflection of the national position. Not to actively lend support to the campaign is to give up an area of power for our social, political and cultural regeneration. It is a battle that we cannot afford to lose.

Towards this end the following demands are made:

1) A full-time permanent secretary to be appointed to the programme.

2) A full-time permanent researcher to be appointed to the programme.

3) The BBC recognises the programme within the permanent structure and format of BBC Radio London.

4) A budget to be allocated which will enable the presenters to make programmes which meet the needs of the black community.

Send letters of support to: The Black Londoners Action Committee, c/o Branksea Street, Fulham, London SW6.

Two tokens in one: the only black and the only woman reporter…

Juliet Alexander interviewed

Juliet Alexander was a reporter on the Hackney Gazette in East London for five years. At her initial interview the editor said that taking her on meant that he was killing two minorities in one. He was joking. She is interviewed by Geoffrey Sheridan.

I started at 18, when most people in the office were young, left of centre, and anti-racist. Being black didn't affect what I did at the beginning – that was in 1975. Being a junior reporter meant that I had to do all the crap that was going. Even after I had been on the paper for a few years, if a kid drowned or something like that, I was the one who went to see the family to get a picture of the kid. That was mainly because I was female. Yet in an area that is a quarter black there was no way I could cover all the black stories. And there was no reason why I should go out on those stories, with a few exceptions.

An obvious case was Maurice Hope, the light middleweight world champion, from Antigua. A reporter went out to interview him, and he couldn't understand a word that Maurice said. His mother had an even heavier accent. So I was taken along. Maurice was anti-white before he won the world championship and the white press had ignored him. He said in the interview that the *Hackney Gazette* was the only paper that had given him any publicity, apart from the *West Indian World.*

Some blacks would only deal with me, such as Eddie Grant, who set up the first black recording studio, and Pastor Morris, who does the Finsbury Park Carnival. I covered news from the estates and word went round like wild fire that Juliet did housing stories, so there were lots of blacks there, but whites, too. They found it hard to separate the fact that I was a reporter from the fact that I was black, which is as it should be, I think.

Before I went on to the *Gazette* there had been trouble at

Dalston police station. A black youth had his head flushed down the loo. It was felt it might do the police some good if they got to know a black person in a different way. I probably did very good PR work on behalf of black people. The only blacks the police met were those they arrested. Meeting a black person on professional terms was as much an experience for them as it was for me.

Sexism and racism

In fact their attitude was of a bunch of men to a woman, rather than to a black. They were incredibly sexist in some cases, and began with the attitude: 'This silly little girl can't do her job, so we'll go out of our way to help her.' Realising that not all blacks wear woolly caps, there was a slight shift in their thinking. With another reporter they'd say: 'Two niggers were picked up for mugging an old lady.' With me it was: 'Two muggers were picked up...' But sometimes they'd say 'mugger' meaning 'nigger'. It was ingrained.

Hackney ——————— FOUNDED 1864
——————— Gazette
FRIDAY, JULY 30, 1982
No. 15,885   AND NORTH LONDON ADVERTISER   12p

Racism came from outside the office, not inside. This man called Sid rang up one day complaining about blacks vandalising his estate. 'He didn't mind blacks,' he said, but it was obvious he did. That's what a lot of people who rang up said. 'I'm not racist, but...' I told Sid his experience was really awful — I was doing my middle-class Tory lady bit. I invited him over to the paper and met him at reception. He recognised my voice, dropped his head in his hands, and called himself 'Sid the Shit'. We had a long talk. There was one of those phone calls every day.

The paper's policy led to abusive phone calls. We followed the NUJ policy of not putting in someone's colour unless it was material to the story, such as a black musician where his colour is part of the description of what he does. We would never put emotive terms into the headline or the introduction of an article. The North London branch of the NUJ was very militant and backed the union's guidelines. The editor agreed with that. But if it was common knowledge that someone was black — if the evening papers had said so — we'd get abusive phone calls wanting to know why we didn't call 'a spade a spade'.

Striking against racism

We had a walk-out over racism. During the Greater London Council elections in 1977 a reporter noticed that an advert for a National Front meeting was due to go into the paper. The management said they couldn't remove it. It was an immediate decision to go out on strike. I was doing the front-page lead article that day. I put it in my bag and walked out. We were out for three days, and picked up a hell of a lot of signatures supporting our action. We normally completely ignored NF meetings. The only time we mentioned them was in unfavourable terms – who they'd beaten up that week. In elections we gave details of all the candidates except the NF's. We simply said they were standing two candidates, or however many it was.

Before I went to the *Gazette* it had given coverage to Derek Day – a leading NF member – and to tenants in Hoxton, which was a fascist base. Things changed a bit. When Day's address was published in the paper, because his son was involved in a court case, he came down to the office, distressed the receptionist, and demanded to see the editor. I volunteered to go down. He was ranting and raving. He came up to me, nose to nose. 'I'm Derek Day,' he yelled. 'I'm racist and proud of it.' He described the *Gazette* in unglowing terms, tore the paper in shreds, and threw it over me. I thanked him for his comment and excused myself.

As far as the NF was concerned, we were a 'Nigger-loving Commie rag', which is what they sprayed on the building. When flags were put up for the Jubilee, someone came into the office to lower them. 'We had no right to fly the British flag,' we were told.

(Juliet Alexander left the *Hackney Gazette* to work on the BBC Radio London programme *Black Londoners*. She now works in TV in the Midlands.)

Race, reporting and the riots

Phil Cohen

Certain common features of press coverage of the 1981 riots and recent race relations stories shed revealing light on the media's political role. It is worth identifying these before looking at the coverage in greater detail.

One noticeable thread running through media reports is the lack of any explanation for the events – indeed an assumption that no explanations exist. As far as Fleet Street is concerned these 'disturbances' happen out of the blue and have no history. That is why it is always necessary to set up Royal Commissions and tribunals of inquiry to 'discover' the causes of these sudden outbursts. Rioting as a conscious expression of long-held grievances or feelings is discounted. Instead media reporting harps on diversionary theories such as that of the 'mob rabble', the 'criminal element' and the 'outside conspiracy'. The latter idea was introduced very soon after the event (this was true of Southall, April 1979, and Brixton, April 1981) only to be discounted later as without foundation. But it served the immediate diversionary purpose.

The real 'conspiracy' takes place between sections of the media and the police who skilfully exploit their own record of events to suit their own purposes. Journalists are accomplices (usually willing) in this manipulation. The fact that it is often crime reporters who are sent out to cover riots or race stories is a comment in itself on how news editors see their significance. Crime reporters lean heavily on Scotland Yard as a key source of news and information (many work directly from the press room at the Yard which has all the necessary facilities such as press telephones). To consistently display the annoying habit of checking with other sources – or showing scepticism towards the police account – is to court disfavour with the Yard. To maintain their 'hot line' to the police reporters are forced to develop an uncritical attitude towards police information and

* Phil Cohen formerly covered race relations as a reporter with the Morning Star. He is now a journalist with the Legal Action Group Bulletin.

only provide a cursory balance with accounts from other sources.

This process can be seen year after year in the build-up coverage to the Notting Hill Carnival, in reporting the annual crime figures and during investigations into events such as the Deptford fire. One *Times* reporter told me that Scotland Yard had complained to her editor during a meeting that her coverage was too anti-police. She was asked by him to 'correct' the balance in future.

In the view of one civil rights solicitor, who has extensive experience of US riots, 'Fleet Street reporting reveals a sharpening edge of racism and a deeply incestuous relationship with Scotland Yard that proceeds unchecked.' Referring to the recent controversy over police crime figures, she asks: 'Do the stories represent the independent judgement of reporters and editors or do they instead give prominence to officially sanctioned and judiciously-timed police leakages so that public opinion becomes, on examination, suspiciously close to other products of Scotland Yard's press office, providing its own justification for its own actions?' (Gareth Peirce, *Guardian*, March 15, 1982).

Scarman blames media

Another diversionary tactic is to blame the media for worsening the riots, rather than looking at the specificity of how they report them. This is usually aimed at the TV channels with the strong implication that pictures of street clashes have a 'copycat' effect on those people (normally young) watching. Lord Scarman in his report on Brixton responded to this notion with four paragraphs out of his 154 pages, devoted to the media. Without a shred of evidence he maintains that 'the media, particularly the broadcasting media, do in my view bear a responsibility for the escalation of the disorders (including the looting) in Brixton on Saturday April 11 and for their continuation the following day, and for the imitative element in the later disorders elsewhere.' He urges editors and producers to ensure 'balance' in the coverage of riots while making a vague reference to criticism that the media do not report areas such as Brixton 'fairly'.

This view of media responsibility was echoed by former Tory Attorney General Peter Rawlinson in the Lords debate on Scarman. He said the BBC especially bore 'a substantial degree of responsibility' for escalating the riots and that there was a blurring of the distinction between reporting and commenting and a decline in the amount of news reporting. In addition to the fact that Scarman's own timetable showed the rioting well under way by the time BBC cameras arrived in Brixton, an independent study from the

British Film Institute Research Unit commissioned by the BBC and the IBA showed that less than 10 per cent of teenagers watch any kind of television news anyway. And groups of youths interviewed in cities where riots took place said television had not influenced them.

There is, however, more point in the statement by Eric Moonman, who produced a Contemporary Affairs briefing on 'copycat hooligans', that 'the media must bear some of the responsibility for the prevalence of stereotyping, particularly of different racial groups and of the police, by the way they are portrayed in dramatic presentations'. There seems little doubt that the media spends far more time responding to events than to promoting education and research into the causes of social tension.

All these threads can be observed running through newspaper coverage of the St Paul's, Bristol riot of April 1980, the Brixton riots of April 1981, the riots in Liverpool, Manchester and elsewhere that followed in July − and in the reporting of crime figures in March 1982 which contained a racial breakdown of 'violent theft'. The analysis that follows of some of that newspaper coverage does not pretend to be comprehensive and is merely intended to give a flavour of what was written.

VIOLENCE RULES IN NINE HOURS OF SIEGE TERROR

The Bristol Evening Post of Thursday April 3, 1980 carried the front page headline 'Violence Rules In Nine Hours of Siege Terror' together with smaller headlines, 'Now 300 police in riots vigil' and 'They just went wild'. The latter was tied to an interview with the owner of the Black and White cafe and his brother after the police raid for drugs which sparked off the protest, but the headline gives no clue to this. No mention is made of the savage police dogs used in the raid and the fact that the advice of the community liaison officer was ignored. The story is written as if there had never been police harassment of people in St Paul's. If it had cared to investigate *The Post* would have heard from local black people how several of their clubs had been closed down and how they saw the raid as yet another attack on what little community facilities they had.

Headlines of 'horror'

In the main story St Paul's is called 'the immigrant district', and in a statement Bristol's police chief says he thinks he should have used more men on the raid, not less. Characteristic of such statements, he says he was not aware of any tension between police and residents and does not think the fighting 'typical of the people of St Paul's. I am sure most of them would abhor what happened last night'. Inside on pages two and three we see the headlines 'War On The Streets', 'Counting The Cost Of Mob Rule' and 'Residents Tell Of Riot Horror'. There is just one story headed 'We Knew This Would Happen – Resident' with black shopkeepers and community leaders firmly putting the blame on police behaviour, and a short piece telling us that CRE chairman David Lane was due in Bristol to 'try to piece together the reasons for the explosion of violence'.

Turning to Brixton 1981, the *Sun* for Saturday April 11 is front-paged 'Battle of Brixton' and a subhead says '100 black youths in clash with the cops.' The main story starts 'A mob of 100 black youths battled with police in a London street last night' and inside it ends with 'Brixton, the heart of Britain's West Indian community, is known to its inhabitants as 'The Front Line'. 'It is notorious for muggings, assaults and murders.' This is typical of the racist nonsense that the *Sun* churns out day after day. It delights in insulting black people by describing them as unthinking 'mobs' who are violent by nature. Since *Sun* reporters only venture into areas like Brixton when there is a juicy 'riots' story for them there is no way they would know what 'The Front Line' is really like, and no reason why those who live there should tell them. Why co-operate one day with people who will insult you the next?

'Troublemakers' blamed

The *Sunday People*, the next day, had a front page shouting 'Brixton Erupts', and '97 Police Injured In Mob Riot Of Fire And Looting,' with a picture of a police officer bleeding. It also had a statement from Metropolitan police Commissioner Sir David McNee, who claimed that 'unconfirmed reports indicated that troublemakers from elsewhere' may have been behind the riots. 'This aspect will be carefully investigated,' he said enigmatically and added that it was almost a year since the Bristol riots and there could be a connection. 'Whatever the reason there would be no excuse for the mindless violence,' he concluded.

Sunday People

APRIL 12 1981   No 5177   20p

97 police injured in mob riot of fire and looting

BRIXTON ERUPTS

BLOODIED . . . a police casualty.

SMOULDERING Brixton erupted in flames and violence last night. Hundreds of black and white youths clashed with police in bloody battles.

At least 97 police were injured as they faced a hail of petrol bombs, bricks and bottles.

70 arrested in night of terror

CLOSING PRICES

THE NEW STANDARD
Incorporating the Evening News

Monday, April 13, 1981.   Price 12p.

Whitelaw orders a major inquiry

WHY, WHY, WHY?

HOME SECRETARY Mr William Whitelaw this afternoon announced a full-scale inquiry into the weekend riots in Brixton.

The inquiry—to be held in public—will be headed by Lord Scarman, a High Court judge since 1961.

Mr Whitelaw, announcing the inquiry in a Commons statement, said: "The police will continue to do their duty to maintain the law on the streets of London, and in this they are entitled to the full support of Parliament and the nation."

Of the rioting, Mr Whitelaw said: "Whatever the grievances individuals or communities feel they suffer, such violence—from whatever quarter it comes—cannot and will not be condoned."

Ulster MP Mr Enoch Powell commented tersely: "Will the Home Secretary and the Government bear in mind

---

THE TIMES

Monday April 13 1981
No. 60,901
Price twenty pence

Mr Whitelaw expected to announce inquiry into Brixton riots today

After three days of violence in Brixton Mr William Whitelaw, Home Secretary, is expected to announce today that a government inquiry is to be set up into the riots. He reported back to Mrs Margaret Thatcher yesterday after touring the area. Tension remained high in the district last night as running battles developed between police and black youths. By late last night there had been 242 casualties and 168 arrests.

Running battles in streets for second night

BRIXTON LAID WASTE—a lone fireman damps down the debris.

Notice how the police quickly plant the idea of outside conspir-
ators, as well as labelling the trouble 'mindless'. Both are designed
to deny any possibility that Brixton's black population knows its
own mind and had genuine grievances, top of the list of which is, of
course, Sir David's own police force. Yet the truth about Bristol and
Brixton was that the people living in those areas revolted against
oppressive policing as well as other social and economic injustices.

The Observer had the headline 'The Night Brixton Burned' and
a sub-head 'Bloody Clashes As Rioters Rampage On Streets Of
London' beside a huge picture of a blazing police van and a dramatic
shot of a policeman's face streaming with blood. The story which is
detailed and relatively unsensational by contrast claimed that 'most
of the black anger yesterday was directed against about 20 young
white plain clothes policemen who had spent the day in the district'.
A police spokesperson, in an attempt to give some motive to police
action, then uttered the immortal words: 'Nobody rules the streets
of London, Brixton or even Railton Road except the Metropolitan
Police'.

In Bristol the police withdrew — but only because they were
outnumbered, not because they thought it would help the situation.
In Brixton there were many community leaders and councillors who
tried to get the police to withdraw as a first step to easing the
tension. But the police refused. Little of that was reported in the
media, perhaps because senior officers had decided at the start that
they were going to 'rule the streets' and the media obediently
supported them.

Ironically there was also a page three story headed 'Southall
Riot Police Are Cleared' which says that 'it is virtually certain that
no action is to be taken against any police officers after nearly 30
complaints about police behaviour during the Southall disturbances
two years ago'.

The *Daily Telegraph* for Monday April 13 carried the front-page
headline 'Looting Gangs Roam Brixton' and 'Teenage Mobs Pour
Out To Bombard Police'. Over the picture of an overturned car is
the strapline 'The hellish sounds of riot — fire alarms, police sirens,
breaking glass, the cries of "pig".' There was a stern warning from
Sir David McNee that there would be no 'no-go' areas in London
and he said police 'had put a lot of effort into race relations' in the
area — evidently not enough.

Nowhere in that interview is he pressed about 'Operation
Swamp '81', the secret saturation policing exercise by units of plain
clothes police which involved stopping and searching hundreds of
local people during the week before the riot. It was that straw that
broke the camel's back as far as the youth of Brixton was concerned

– but Sir David is not asked why no one in the community was told about the operation at such a sensitive time for race relations.

Shape of things to come?

Inside are two pages of pictures with the glory headlines 'Blood Flows In Brixton's Orgy Of Violence' and 'Scars Of Battle In The Riot-torn Streets'. An editorial backs the police and compares Brixton – 'the law of the Molotov cocktail' – with the election of hunger-striker Bobby Sands in Northern Ireland – 'the law of the gun'. Hints of alarm at the dropping of further prosecutions arising from the Bristol riots are made and the editorial ends by recommending an inquiry to look into whether there were 'organised mischief makers at work on Saturday... Inquiries can only determine facts. Part of the trouble in Brixton, indeed in "race relations", is that there are people who will not accept facts'.

The *Daily Mirror* of the Monday had a striking banner headline across front and back pages, 'The Shape Of Things To Come' with a huge picture of street confrontation between stone-throwing black and white youths and police with riot shields. The paper quotes Haringey community relations officer Jeff Crawford saying the trouble will spread to Birmingham and Manchester. Black leaders support the youths while David Lane calls the events 'deplorable'. Police chiefs accused 'agitators' of preparing petrol bombs in advance and spoke of white photographers, not press, 'who snapped every move' the police made. *The Times* of the Monday had a sober page one headline 'Mr Whitelaw Expected To Announce Inquiry Into Brixton Riots Today'.

The whole of page four is then given over to Brixton coverage with eye-witness reports, an article on the way Handsworth in Birmingham may have averted such trouble with community policing, and one young black saying rioting was the only way to express feelings of despair.

The *Morning Star*, alone among the papers, blames police harassment for the riots with the headline 'Brixton Points The Finger' and a statement from Lambeth Communist Party describing the police as like 'an occupying army'.

The *Evening Standard* screamed 'Why, Why, Why?' on its front page with a story saying 'the object of one police inquiry is to find out if the riots were a spontaneous reaction by the black community of Brixton protesting at police harassment or if they were deliberately started'. Inside there is a two-page headline 'Days Of Hatred That Destroyed Brixton', changed in a later edition to 'Violent

★ Morning Star

Apartheid's
victim: p4

6578/14343 20p ★ ★   INCORPORATING THE DAILY WORKER   MONDAY APRIL 13 1981

Police harassment ● no hope of jobs ● decaying housing

Brixton points the finger

By DAVE LLOYD

BESIEGED and battered Brixton yesterday demanded urgent action to stop provocative police methods.

As clashes continued last night after a weekend of violence local leaders drew attention to the appalling unemployment and social problems in this area of London.

Lambeth council's Labour leader Ted Knight said that there were 17,900 jobless in the borough.

"1,550-1,800 of these are under twenty and have never had a job. The prospects are virtually nil," he said. Up to 50 per cent of Brixton's youth unemployed are black.

Mr. Knight added that Lambeth council had warned the government three months ago that "it was on the edge of a time bomb which would explode —now it has."

Last night's violence, after an attempted arrest, was further proof of this.

Mr. Knight hit out at the way the police had saturated the area and refuted claims that the incidents were "race riots."

There was no race conflict here, he said. "No black and white people were fighting each other. The conflict was one with

Police methods blamed

Morning Star Reporter

THE ONLY "outside elements" causing trouble in Brixton at the weekend were the police—including outside units drafted in—and the Special Patrol Group, Lambeth Community Party declared yesterday, rejecting police claims that outside agitators were at work.

"It is the police methods and the blatant racism that are to blame for the events," said the Communists.

"The police are using methods that have been condemned by community leaders, MPs, trade unionists, the leader of Lambeth council and the Lambeth working party on police-community relations.

"The problems will only be solved when the underlying causes are tackled—the unemployment, especially among black Britons, the bad housing, the lack of facilities resulting from the cuts in the inner-city

programme set up to prevent problems of this kind.

"Further, a police force that behaves like an occupying army is no help to Lambeth."

The Communists demand:
Immediate withdrawal of the SPG and the extra police forces.
A top-level public inquiry using the working party report as major evidence.
A police force that is answerable to the community they are meant to serve and protect—
a first step would be to put the Metropolitan police under the control of the Greater London Council, and not the Home Office.

The removal from the borough of the headquarters of the NF who will exploit the situation.

The restoration of cuts in local government spending, and the inner-city and job creation programmes, with especially, more funds for local recreation centres.

Hours That Destroyed Brixton' in order that a running logo could be introduced on several pages containing a black face and the words 'the streets of hate'. The *Standard* coverage was merely the culmination of that paper's well-known anti-black anti-working class stance on most issues. It consistently uses its monopoly of newspapers in London to sensationalise issues and directly attack progressive bodies like the left wing GLC as well as to mount scare stories about black crime. Again it lapped up the police's 'conspiracy' theory.

Government challenged

Further headlines from the *Daily Telegraph* of July 1981 continue the same treatment. These include 'Police Face Mobs Again' (July 6), 'London Looting Campaign – Imitation Riots' (July 8) and 'Britain's Night Of Anarchy' (July 11) with a story: 'Hunt for the Four Horsemen... Special Branch detectives are trying to identify the "Four Horsemen" of the rioting epidemic... the four hooded men *who it has been established* were present at major incidents in Southall, Liverpool and Manchester'. The riots also put pressure on the highest levels of government with Mrs Thatcher saying it was 'her most worrying time' and the government was forced to make some response. 'Riots Put Pressure On Cabinet To Review Economic Strategy' said the *Financial Times* of July 13.

Gareth Pierce has pointed out how Fleet Street paved the way for the crime figures issued by Scotland Yard on March 11, 1982, with a number of alarming stories in the *Daily Mail* and the *Daily*

Express spotlighting the rise in 'muggings' and linking them directly with young blacks. (Stuart Hall et al in *Policing The Crisis*, Macmillans) have analysed the origins and development of the racist category of 'the mugger', as part of the machinery of a strong state in a period of economic crisis). On the day the figures were released, containing a racial breakdown of just three per cent of crimes relating to robbery (of which only 0.9 per cent could be called 'mugging'), *The Mail* had the headline 'Black Crime: The Alarming Figures' and other papers were headed 'Yard Reveals Race Link In Street Crime Explosion' and 'Black Muggers Blamed By Yard'. The impression was given that the crimes referred to were violent and the victims were mostly white, elderly females. In fact a Home Office research official Michael Pratt, in a study of 'muggings' in London found that 59 per cent involved no injury and 81 per cent of the victims were male. The largest number of victims were in the 21-30 age group.

The overall meaning of such coverage is that black equals crime. Although Scotland Yard claimed that 'there is a demand for this information from the public and from the media on behalf of the public' it merely helped Fleet Street to bolster the myths perpetuated all the year round concerning black people. Once again the police and the media worked in concert to orchestrate a racist theory. As with the riots the reports in newspapers and broadcasting were few that sought to dissect the mythology and reveal the underlying racism.

Racism on television: bringing the colonies back home

Tony Freeth

When the safari hunters from the BBC or TV companies drive into Brixton or Brent they've already decided what they want to say. Out come the cameras and the anxious directors, looking over their shoulders for trouble; out come the long zoom lenses to capture the people but not to get too close; and out come the bubbling production assistants, eager to please everyone and prove themselves by chatting up a Rastafarian to give an interview on camera. Safari tales in the bar afterwards − they bagged a real lion this time.

Often it really is like this. Gone are the pith helmets, but essentially colonial attitudes of mind dominate, and racist preconceptions mediate the whole process. And these attitudes are directly reflected in the images from which TV programmes are constructed.

A grammar of images

It's easy to spot a TV programme about what they call the Black Problem or the Race Problem. There are the long telephoto shots of young blacks in the street, and the ultra big close-ups in interviews. There are the pans across inner city decay, and the shots of rubbish in the lifts. I sometimes wonder why they go out at all − they could just as well use the out-takes from the last time. It's a vocabulary of images which, through constant repetition, gets into the audiences way of thinking. For white people who don't know black people it

* Tony Freeth is a freelance film producer and director who works mainly in television. A former secretary of Paddington Campaign Against Racism, he is an active member of Campaign Against Racism in the Media, and was part of the group who made CARM's 'Open Door' programme 'It Ain't Half Racist, Mum!'

defines what black people are supposed to be like, and this is invariably reinforced by the commentary. It's an inner city disaster area and the ingredients haven't changed. Over a long telephoto shot of black people in the street — from a *Newsnight* on The Scarman Report. Or from an earlier BBC documentary, *Race: The Way We Live Now:* '… in Brent white families are outnumbered three to one by blacks' (my italics). Black people aren't thought of as having families, and the situation is always seen as one of threat from black people. Many BBC producers seem to be fighting out the Battle of Rorke's Drift in their heads every time they deal with issues involving black people.

Another favourite image is of a white policeman being friendly to a group of black children. The policeman is often described as being 'The PC Dixon of…'. It's an image which I've seen in at least four different documentaries, and it's worth thinking about why directors choose to shoot it so often.

The images and commentary, constantly reinforcing racist ideas, aren't shoved in our faces. They're just woven seamlessly into the continuous flow of TV images. They're a powerful learning process for white audiences who, through lack of alternative information, have few critical ways of looking at television about black people.

What I want to emphasise is that there's nothing 'neutral', 'balanced' or 'objective' about the way TV portrays black people. It's a highly structured image and results from conscious selections by the people who make the programmes, working in institutions where there is an underlying racism. Of course there are some exceptions — black people working in television who refuse to be used as collaborators, and white people also who are against the colonial consensus. My own experience, as a freelance director making a programme for BBC schools, in a small way shows what many of the institutional attitudes are.

Scene: why prejudice?

I didn't choose the title — I would have preferred 'Why Racism?' — or the context, a group of students at a London comprehensive school. But, after talking to my producer, I felt confident that the sort of programme proposed could usefully encourage people, particularly white school students, to begin to question their own racial attitudes. My producer was in complete support of the sort of approach I wanted to take. However my confidence in the project was not reinforced by my meeting with the Head of Schools or the

Executive Producer. In many ways their anxious and embarrassed approach to the subject, and the Head of Schools attempts to steer the programme away from white racism as the major problem to look at, are typical of the sort of attitudes in the BBC.

The first thing my producer and I were told was that 'It's a very sensitive issue, and our advice from teachers is that they've just about got the problem licked'. (This was after St Pauls and before Brixton, Toxteth etc.) We were then told that we should realise that 'There is terrible prejudice between West Indians and Asians' (so it's not really a white problem at all!); that 'It's a human problem' (nothing to do with history, politics or economics, or anything like that!); and that 'Many black people imagine prejudice when it doesn't really exist'. (So racism's not a problem at all, just a figment of black people's imagination!) When I said that all the black people I knew who said they'd suffered discrimination had, in my view, actually suffered discrimination, he said 'I don't actually know any black people, but I do know some Polish immigrants'. He's now retired, but his clones live on in the BBC.

During filming we wanted to use some clips from racist comedy shows. Thames refused to let us have *Love Thy Neighbour* or *The Jim Davidson Show*. The BBC did not let us have a clip of *It Ain't Half Hot, Mum!* The man responsible for this said he didn't know what the fuss was about — 'the leading actor loves Indians, in fact he thinks the British should never have left India'.

When we got to the first cut of the film, the Executive Producer came to see it. He looked a bit put out when we got to the bit with Cecil Gutzmore from the Black Peoples Information Centre talking about African history and culture. At the end he said he thought we should cut him out. 'Why?', we asked. 'Because he's a bit of a stereotype of himself'. 'I don't understand what you mean'. Embarrassed silence. We kept him in.

The film is based round a group of highly intelligent, and articulate school students, two third of whom are black. The Head of Schools saw the programme the day before transmission. I was told that his only comment was 'I think they're the stupidest bunch of kids I've ever come across'. At a later screening he said 'I still feel I'm being got at'. Maybe the programme really was worthwhile.

The BBC doesn't call black people 'niggers' anymore. In general TV doesn't confront us with racist banner headlines like the popular press. It all takes place in an atmosphere of smiling, middle-class gentility, an air of righteous indignation if confronted with charges of racism. No one in TV shouts racist abuse at black people, they just hardly ever employ black people above a certain level in the hierarchy. No one in TV physically assaults black people, they

London Weekend Television

A shot from BBC's Mind Your Language

simply feed us on a diet of 'Blacks are the Problem' and a constant reiteration of all the old stereotypes — a daily massage for white racism. Underneath the bland exteriors of most TV executives all the colonial attitudes survive. They would have us believe that the nasty thing called racism has nothing to do with them — it's all perpetuated by the British working class. My own view is that if we want to know who is really perpetuating racism in our society we have to look particularly at the upper and middle classes. The employers who discriminate on a massive scale against black people. Governments who have passed one racist Immigration Bill after another. Doctors who have sterilised Asian women without their informed consent. Chief Constables who have consistently failed to protect people against racist attacks and have failed to deal with racism in their own forces. And last but not least the media professionals.

Of course there's no denying working-class racism. What's important is understanding where the responsibility lies. The tragedy of many white working-class racists is that they haven't understood how the ways that black people and their cultures have been discriminated against. The process has also been colonial. Great Britain has been described as the last colony in the British Empire. This isn't only true at the economic and political level, it operates crucially at the level of culture. And it's worked against white as well as black working class communities. The destruction of white working-class cultures has been both insidious and vicious. It's operated through a whole range of techniques from direct attack through patronage to incorporation of certain 'approved' aspects of working-class culture in a denatured form with all content of 'resistance' removed.

The media has been a crucial part of this process. In my view an essential step towards building a non-racist society is an affirmation of white working-class cultures. I don't believe they're inherently racist, I think that they were co-opted in to the colonial process in a way which has now left people with a great loss of identity. We were taught to be proud to be British, and what being British meant was being rulers of a big Empire with all the racism which that entailed. White people need to understand that there are ways of being proud of their own cultures without involving the whole imperial, nationalistic and racist nonsense as well.

The assault on culture

Racism on the defensive is always changing its forms and techniques, and one of the main targets for the current racist backlash is culture. Throughout colonialism culture has been a particular focus for racism, from the days when attempts were made to prevent people from speaking their own languages and contempt was poured on all the forms of people's own cultures. In Ireland as well as Africa and the Caribbean the patterns were similar. Colonialism has always felt threatened by people's own cultures, and the same is true today. White racism has suffered a whole series of defeats during this century, and one of the key strengths of these victories has been the reaffirmation from the USA, and from Africa and India of black people's cultures.

The tactics of colonialism have a dual nature – the smiling face of white racism and its approval of black people who deny their own cultures, coupled with the knee-in-the-groin-behind-closed-doors approach to people who resist the patterns of colonialism. And within this, there are aspects of black cultures which are approved, from the stereotyped 'sense of rhythm' or 'happy disposition' to the adulation of the American Blues.

The type of film making related to this is 'cultural tourism'. It comes from the traditions of colonial anthropology, and the nineteenth century obsession with collecting cultural artifacts. It feeds on ideas of 'exotica' and cultural voyeurism. On TV the 'World About Us' often reflects this tradition 'The National Geographic Magazine' of the box. The effect is to patronise black people, to de-historicise their cultures, and to separate them from anti-colonial struggle.

But many of the ways TV deals with black cultures comes as a more direct assault. An aspect of a culture is put 'on trial'. White TV executives and pundits are the judge and jury, often with a few token black middle-class people to avoid charges of bias. Arranged marriages are a prime example. Because of TV's obsession with arranged marriages, it's about the only thing that many white people know about Asian cultures except that 'they eat curry'. Nearly always looked at from a position of assumed cultural superiority and with the underlying assumption that it's wrong, TV hands out its arrogant judgements.

In a similar way young people of West Indian origin are nearly always described as 'searching for identity'. As used by white people it's nearly always a patronising phrase. How often do you hear it said that white people should be searching for a new identity — a non-racist identity?

No positive images

An important way that TV works on us as an audience is by giving us positive images of what we might do or what we could be like. For black people there are very few positive images, except in carefully selected contexts — athletes, musicians, and the culturally 'approved'. Black people obviously have the right to control and construct images of themselves and their cultures. This demand is at the moment centred around Channel Four, with maybe some hope of fulfilment. It must obviously extend to the whole of television, and to white as well as black cultures. Britain has always been a multi-cultural society, and the right for all working-class communities to control their own media images has always been denied. The issues are deeply political, and becoming increasingly important in a world where the technological means of cultural colonialism are becoming every day more sophisticated.

Writing racism

With Drama and Comedy the underlying attitudes tend to be the same. Again the racist jokes, like anti-Irish jokes, coming from a colonial history, and the racial sit-coms riddles with stereotypes and one-dimensional characters. Look at the script for *The Jim Davidson Show* and you'll frequently see the phrase 'Black Biz' — that's the cue for our Jim to do his black imitations.

When it comes to Drama it's also worth looking at the process of construction. How do white writers go about constructing black characters? For the most part they know very few black people, and certainly haven't grown up in any black culture. So when they sit down and think about what a black character would do or feel, all they've got to go on for the most part are all the preconceptions and stereotypes which, as white people living in a racist society, we all learn. The other source of models for these writers are films and TV programmes, written for the most part by other white writers... this isn't to say that all the characters will turn out as racial stereotypes. Many of the more 'liberal' writers will consciously write characters 'against' these stereotypes – black characters who are good, clean, honest, hard-working... But the writing can only be relative to stereotypes. The characters live in the same landscape of racist stereotypes because the writers don't understand the cultures from which their characters are supposed to come. The ATV series 'Walcott' illustrates this well. Written by white writers, one from the USA, the series lay squarely inside the US 'Blaxploitation' genre. Though supposedly set in Britain, the characters and situations had almost nothing to do with the black cultures and communities in this country. The black characters were written in a 'Shaft' and 'Superfly' fantasy world from the USA, and I'd guess that these have little to do with real black American culture. All the situations and characters were woven from a fabric of racist stereotypes and racist anti-stereotypes. It must have cost about a million pounds. That's a pretty heavy investment in racism.

Black writers

In a paper for the Edinburgh TV Festival in 1977 Sue Woodford and Margaret Walters, in recognising the problem of white writers writing black parts, suggested that white writers should write characters which should then be cast with black actors. At least we'd get fully rounded characters, neither racist stereotypes nor anxious liberal anti-stereotypes. But the trouble with this is that it robs the characters of their culture and hence of a true identity. It may be a better solution for most white writers, and it may give work to black actors, but if it is the only change it would simply reinforce the present system of cultural racism.

The solution to the problem is obvious. Employ more black writers. TV producers keep telling us that 'there aren't enough good writers with TV experience'. If they wanted them they could get them. Of course many black writers don't have TV experience because TV doesn't often employ them. But at a time when there is an important new black theatre emerging, it's ridiculous to suggest that good black writers aren't available.

The bad-apple-in-the-barrel theory of racism

Over the last few years television has spent much more effort in sophisticating its techniques of defence against charges of racism than in dealing with the racism itself. The almost universal theory of racism in TV circles is the bad-apple-in-the-barrel view, which says that there may be a few bad apples in the barrel — the police or media or Management etc. — only get rid of these and everything's going to be okay.

It's a theory which says that racism is never their problem, and that we don't need any fundamental changes in our social institutions. My own view of racism is that, as white people brought up in a racist society, we cannot remain unaffected by it. We need to be involved in a constant process of examining all our assumptions, ideas and feelings. We must mistrust most of our judgements, and unlearn many of our ideas. In the end it is a liberating process because it frees us from the myths, lies, and stereotypes which we were brought up with. But it's a long way from the bad-apple theory which simply involves us in identifying the 'racists'.

One of the consequences for TV of this view of racism is that most white TV executives and producers simply aren't capable of making the right judgements when it comes to programmes about black people. Most of them tell you volubly how they 'bend over backwards to give black people a fair crack of the whip'. Whether they know what nonsense this is or not doesn't really matter. What does matter is the perpetuation of racist attitudes and their constant denials that they exist.

More 'liberal' programmes?

Many people will object that I've been too hard on TV. The idea that TV still lives in a world of colonial attitudes is contradicted by an increasing number of more 'liberal' programmes. For example people cite LWT's *Skin*, ATV's *An Arranged Marriage* and BBC's *Neighbours*. Of course there have been some more progressive programmes, and even very rarely programmes where there have been black people in key positions of control. But overwhelmingly it's white people who are in control of these programmes, and so decide on the cultural and political emphasis. The cultural 'signature' of these programmes evidently derives from the dominant, white middle-class culture of TV, however 'sympathetic' they may be towards the people they're about.

Over the last few years I've seen a lot of white TV directors and film school students at Caribbean events in London making films about black people. They are very often 'liberal' or even 'socialist', and they frequently win prizes at Film Festivals. I have some respect for a few of them, but for the most part when you ask who they're making films for, or why they're making them in the first place, you get very ambivalent or confused answers. They're almost universally mistrusted by the black people I know. In my view, at the present stage of anti-racist and anti-colonial struggle, people shouldn't make films which are uncommitted. And films shouldn't be made without any form of accountability to the people the films are about.

So where do films like the BBC's *Neighbours* fit in? John Wyver in *City Limits* described it as 'a strong, vital and important film' of which 'the Bristol Arts Unit should be proud'. My own feelings are much more ambivalent. Coming from a fine film-maker like Barrie Gavin I had a feeling of disappointment. In spite of having some strong and positive images, it was a film which managed to take a community which had won a pioneering and major victory in the struggle against racism, and create an image of defeat. At times I had an uncomfortable feeling that for much of the audience it would just be a form of cultural tourism, though I'm sure that wasn't the film-maker's intention.

How did this happen? To me it seemed to have all the hallmarks of a film where many of the people in the film only half-trusted the process, and the people who weren't (many of whom may have had more significant contributions to make) didn't trust the process at all, and so refused to take part. The film did have some strong things in it, and was put under great pressure by the BBC hierarchy, which is a good reason to defend it. But I felt that the film was an unsatisfactory half-way house between cultural tourism and a significant portrait of a community involved in anti-colonial struggle.

If there is to be significant change in the TV image of our black communities, there must be change in the production process. The subjects of such films must have an editorial role in the film at the conceptual, production and editing stages of the process. And, even more important, there must be more black film-makers.

Within the way that TV makes programmes at present, it's very difficult for film-makers to give up any editorial control. Except of course in the BBC's 'access' slot, *Open Door*. I'm not usually interested in making access programmes, where the film-maker is entirely at the service of the group involved. All too often this mid-wife role is like assisting at a birth of Siamese Quins where all the quins are arguing with each other while coming out feet first. But I am interested in making films in partnership with groups or individuals who are involved in various struggles. It's a difficult process, and involves both partners having a share of control in the final product. It's a process which must involve full consultation at every stage from planning and developing the ideas through shooting and editing, and distribution. I hope Channel Four may provide a context for this sort of process – they've certainly stated this commitment. What we need to develop is a new contract between film-makers and the people the films are made with, so that films can be 'for' instead of simply 'about' people and their struggles.

This sort of new contract is for the most part impossible inside the present BBC and TV companies. So what's important is to change the structure of television.

Changing television

There are various tactical struggles which are urgent. An end to racist discrimination in employment is a priority, with a setting of definite targets and a positive programme of training in order to achieve these targets. This is important not only because people have a right to non-racist employment practices, but because it should have a significant effect on content.

Employment practices should be non-racist in the cultural sense also. All colonial processes have attempted to incorporate black people as administrators, and TV is no exception. TV has a consistent history of class discrimination as well. Along the dimensions of race, class, sex and culture TV has woven a tangled web of discrimination. And, for the most part, its only response to criticism of its practices is more and more defensive justifications.

The few areas of the media, like *Black Londoners*, whose content is actually controlled by black people, must be defended against continued harassment through lack of adequate resources as well as direct racism. Programmes like *Skin*, which pretend to represent black people, but are wholly controlled by white people, should be changed or closed down. Sometimes they do good programmes, but they ain't half soft on white racism. In the longer term we must work to change control of the BBC and ITV. What we need is a system of direct, democratic control of television, which is independent of Government, and which properly represents our different cultures.

'Wolcott' ... 1 — the black view

Imruh Caesar, Henry Martin,
Colin Prescod, Menelik Shabaz

Not since *Roots* by Alex Hayley have we been treated to the kind of black television blitz that ATV's *Wolcott* gave us from January 13 through to January 16, 1981. And, in its January issue, *West Indian World* boasted that we had at last in Britain, our first real black TV star in George Harris. George was the star of *Wolcott*, a four part cops and robbers drama which swamped for three nights solid with a double dose (2 hours) on the final night. Wolcott aimed to provide the nation with an acute, closely observed, but entertaining picture of the inner-city, black community — the 'natives' mainly at play, and hardly ever at what you'd call work.

Whose image

So blacks appear to have here, a chance of jobs for black actors, and at last, a chance to see our community portrayed in a multi-faceted kind of way. One supposes that all blacks should be happy about this. And indeed many of us will have been so happy to see ourselves reflected in the great TV eye, which normally looks straight through us like we weren't here, that our first response might have been one of pleasure. And in *Wolcott*, we weren't even painted all black, as so often happens — some of the black characters were painted almost white. (In fact all of them were — as usual). And if the series takes off, soon every nigger could be a star — but at what cost? Stars made in whose image?

For years we've complained that we are grossly under-represented in TV drama, documentary and popular entertainment. And for years our actors have complained that they should be offered full character parts, rather than female servants, studs, and crowd fillers. But if *Wolcott* is a sign of the band-wagons being offered for

* Reprinted from 'Grass Roots' magazine, March 1981

exposure and stardom — we must refuse, and so must our actors.

Wolcott was written and produced to a formula, and although it looked as though it was shot on location in London's black community, it was really not about nor in the interests of any part of the black communities in Britain. Black viewers will have recognised the faces, but not the lines — black youth don't sit in parks chanting 'pig, pig, pig, pig...', when police, black or white walk past. Black viewers will have recognised the ghetto predicaments, but not the events portrayed — we don't have an everyday 'junkie' problem amongst black youth in Britain; nor do we have a black mafia organising youth to mug and stab little old white ladies, for the pittance in their hand-bags.

Condemned

Wolcott is a fictional black cop. But *Wolcott* could also be the best walking advertisement yet devised to attract black people into the police force. It is to be remembered that ever since ex-police chief and star of the Spaghetti House siege, Robert Mark, started a

George William Harris as Wolcott, black detective, and Christine Lahti as Melinda in the Central TV production

campaign to recruit black police in 1972 — spending as much as
£25,000 on it in 1975 — the Force has failed to attract many more
than a couple hundred black police. With *Wolcott* 'we see everything being thrown in to present a recruitment pitch. The bent-
copper is portrayed. Racist coppers are shown, verbally abusing
blacks, even the black in uniform. And *Wolcott* is shown as a man
sensitive to all these abuses and corruptions, and militantly defensive of his blackness — but still with a mind for being a cop. And the
basis on which this trick is turned, is the misrepresentation and
criminalisation of the entire black community. One supposes that
the argument of the nice, white, liberal TV writers and producers,
who made *Wolcott*, must be, that since black youth are all criminal,
then in order to get them policed by other than vindictive, brutal,
white racist cops, black people who care about law and order, and
morality, should consider joining the police. Who are they kidding?
The police in Britain have shown themselves to be *not* accountable
to the black community. That is why we already protest against the
intention to grant extended police powers, as recommended
recently by the Royal Commission on Criminal Procedure. Black
people cannot, in all consciousness, join such a police force. (See,
'Police Against Black People', I.R.R. 1979).

Stereotypes

The producer, Jacky Stoller, is reported to have said, 'I think that
sometimes drama can educate more effectively than documentary.'
Too true — and hence the more serious concern of the present
argument. Ms Stoller believes that she 'learned a lot just from
reading the script and much more from working with the black
actors and on the Hackney locations' (*Guardian*, p.8, 13.1.81). One
doesn't know how much say the black actors had, but the script was
written by two Americans settled in Britain. It showed, Ms Stoller
admits, further, that her art, indeed 'All art, on whatever level, has
to select and emphasise.' So what does this art teach us? She
presented us with a series of stagy, black stereotypes — our youth
were made out to be wayward, muggers and murderous with
parents absent or unable to cope with them, in a community full of
black mafia type gangsters. In order to establish these, we had the
US 'junkie' problem presented as a UK black youth problem — kids
with needles, stretched out in youth club toilets, and dying in their
beds. We had black women represented as either ineffectual or
strong but confused or as prostitutes. We had militant, political
blacks treated dismissively, and shown as irrelevant to the black

youth predicament.

This Americanisation of the black experience in Britain, misrepresented us, criminalised us, and treated us irresponsibly and with disrespect. Even if we go to church, our community still sins all the same. Of course, there were also white baddies portrayed as stereotypes — but we don't have to be as concerned about these misrepresentations, (apart from the celebration of gratuitous violence through them) because the majority white viewers won't be fooled by them as easily. They have a wealth of certain knowledge that all whites are not like that. About blacks, they know nothing but what they are told and what the camera shows them, interpreted through their ignorant fears and their racism.

'Frame-up'

The little details of language, and style, and location, in *Wolcott* were designed to convey realism, but the overall picture they were made to fit into was false. It was, effectively, a frame-up. But what are we being framed-up for? What is the consequence of the entire nation, night after night, being presented with this picture of a degenerate black community. A community which clearly can't be sorted out by one or even a few black cops, no matter how worthy, well-meaning and talented. *Wolcott* is shown to be, all the time, fighting a heroic but finally a losing battle with his people. These criminal and degenerate ghettos can't be cleaned up by even a division of *Wolcotts*. This deeply immoral and confused community is too far gone for even the missionary police, black or white. It's a situation that calls for firm, creative, liberty-taking policing. The picture painted of the fictional black community promotes the idea that between the law abiding citizen and these monsters in the ghetto, stand the police.

Meanwhile in real life the police look like winning the powers to place communities so defined under siege. Blacks are threatened with the real possibility of being prisoners in the streets. From time to time the SPG has done dry runs along these lines. And the nation, indeed the world, having been sold pictures like those painted in *Wolcott*, will have been prepared for the necessity to clamp down even further on blacks — perhaps even with regular police occupations of our communities from time to time. 4 hours of dramatic misrepresentation piled into 3 nights of TV — is bad news for blacks. Very effective because the audience is not used to seeing blacks on TV.

Part of the way out of this situation could involve employing more black writers and producers for TV — but that won't be enough in itself. The new writers and producers black or white must be responsible and respectful of the black community, and conscious of anti-racist imperatives. *Wolcott* happens to have been done by a white production team, but it could have been done by blacks too. Take for example what, at first sight appears to be an unrelated academic exercise carried out about 2 years ago. In 1978 a black sociologist (Afro-Caribbean) came to Britain, researched the Bristol black community, and wrote an apparently liberal and sympathetic Ph.D. on the St. Paul's community. The book was called 'Endless Pressure'. His conclusions could have been the 'scientific' background to the *Wolcott* fiction. He talked about a community of 'saints' and hustlers and teenyboppers, and 'inbetweeners' under such 'endless pressure' that it was unfortunately but undoubtedly a degenerate community. It was this same community that was obliged to rise in April 1980, to defend itself against a massive police occupation which the authorities tried to justify in terms of a 'criminal' black community. Say no more.

'Wolcott' ... 2 – the white producer's view

Wolcott, ATV's homemade answer to all those over-wrought Best Sellers from Hollywood, is somewhat less glossy than its precursors in the Tuesday-through-to-Thursday blockbuster slot. It leans further over towards fact and some of its facts are nasty ones: corruption, violence and racism in a North London community and particularly in its police force.

Winston Churchill Wolcott is your traditional straight baddie-hating cop who has just been promoted from the beat to the CID. To most of the black community he is a 'token nigger' who has sold out to the enemy; to many of his colleagues, he's an uppity one who needs to be told his place. The story line, basic cops v hoodlums and delinquents, is slightly slowed by the necessity to fill in the sociological detail for a television audience mostly used to seeing black actors as shallow stereotypes there just to help the action along.

But the detail is one of *Wolcott*'s strengths. As a Socialist Worker mounts a soapbox to explain to shoppers in Brixton Market that racism fatally divides a working class which should be united and the National Front ripostes with crude slogans of hate, you see the familiar on the screen and realise that there it is unfamiliar. And in the reactions of the blacks there's no romantic response. The argument, you are made to feel, is like that of two dogs squabbling over a bone long since snatched by a third: irrelevant and too late.

The script of *Wolcott* is by two American writers, Barry Wasserman and Patrick Carroll, who settled in Britain some years ago and both of whom live in multiracial areas of London. They wrote it as a screenplay but were unable to find anyone willing to make the film. Eventually the script landed on the desk of Jacky Stoller, a producer with Black Lion Films, a subsidiary of ATV's parent company, ACC.

'I liked it because it is modern; it is about the eighties. The social comment is not window-dressing; it is the background on which the story hinges and which motivates the characters. It is an integral

An interview with Jacky Stoller, by Brenda Polan, reprinted from The Guardian, *January 13, 1981.*

part of a good story and immensely interesting. I learned a lot just from reading the script and much more from working with the black actors and on the Hackney locations,' she says.

Like most intelligent middle-class men and women, Jacky was aware of racism, aware that it was an evil and ready to condemn it. But it was an abstract; through making *Wolcott* she has seen its concrete unreason and malice. 'I want the people who watch *Wolcott* to see that too,' she says. 'I think that sometimes drama can educate more effectively than documentary. Certainly it has the opportunity to educate more people because its audience is wider. But it also has the facility to make people identify with characters from an alien and previously misunderstood group and that can lead to sympathy for the group.'

It can even, she adds with a smile, lead to social and economic change. 'Friends in Oxford told me recently that their cleaning woman had come to them and announced that, since the charlady in Coronation Street was being paid £1.50 an hour, didn't they agree that 75p an hour was rather stingy and ought to be improved upon.'

There has been no attempt in *Wolcott* to twist the truth or make propaganda by making more blacks than should be goodies or more whites baddies – though when Winston Wolcott arrives at his new station, his reception is so hostile, you discover you are anxiously willing just *one* of the whites to be a nice guy. Three give our hero a smile and guilt feelings are relieved.

The Metropolitan force, which does boast 83 people of ethnic minorities on its strength, is said to be none too happy about Wolcott, but there is nothing in it that a careful reading of the newspapers and an evening listening to a South London social worker will not have made you already aware of. 'Of course,' says Jacky, 'you have to heighten some of the dramatic content to make it acceptable on a viewing level. All art, on whatever level, has to select and emphasise.'

Although she would like to produce faction programmes, Jacky is not interested in documentaries. She slipped into drama almost by accident, but it is where she wants to stay. She joined the BBC as a secretary after leaving South Hampstead High School and settled in the drama department with her aim set firmly on production work.

She joined ATV as a production assistant, worked on the first plays to be produced in colour, went freelance and worked for David Susskind in America on those big-budget television specials, and returned to Britain to become a casting director with Yorkshire Television. There she moved on to producing (*Hadleigh, Raffles, The Racing Game*) before leaving Yorkshire for Black Lion Films.

'I discovered,' she says, 'that Yorkshire were not paying me as much as the men doing the same job. They denied it, but I was right.'

A brief marriage when she was 19 left Jacky with a daughter, Louise, to bring up alone. She could not have managed without her old (actually quite young) nanny who stepped in and enabled her to continue her career. Although her fishmonger father would have liked her to go into the family business, she grew up taking equality and the freedom to choose her own future for granted. If she is a feminist, it is the experience of a single woman bringing up a child and pursuing a career which has made her so.

'I would rather like to do a programme which looks closely at women's lives today,' she says. 'There are many problems which women have not yet solved, problems we don't even have a hazy notion of solving. But I am toying with several ideas and approaches.

'Did you realise,' she says, with the air of one who might just have solved this one for herself, 'that this guilt about not devoting enough time to your children is not only exclusively middle-class, but fairly recently acquired as well? Working-class women have always worked; getting the money to feed children came first so how could you feel guilty about it?'

Race, sex and education: press coverage of 'Somebody's Daughter'

Jane King

Somebody's Daughter, a five part television series made in 1978 by ILEA TV for use in Social Studies Courses in Secondary Schools, was shown for the first time to the general public in March 1982 at the ICA's Cinematique, probably the smallest of all London cinemas, for a short limited season only. In Holland, the importance of the issues raised by the film and the quality of their presentation have already been recognised by a showing at peak viewing time on the nation TV network. So why have we had to wait so long for such a limited opportunity to see a work which *Guardian Education* described as 'very sensitvely handled, diligently researched... a highly superior soap-opera (with) no stereotyping or simplistic idealism'?

The answer would seem to lie in the racism of the British popular press. Days before the appearance of the *Guardian* piece, the *Evening Standard*, following a preview for headteachers, proclaimed 'Approved — black and white school sex film' and reported that *Somebody's Daughter* 'was likely to bore and depress its audience'. That was on January 13 1978. The very next day the *Johannesburg Star*'s headline was 'Bristol teachers approve TV film on inter-racial sex', followed by an only minimally edited version of the *Standard*'s account!

Even more sinister was the persistence of almost every British newspaper and periodical, from the *Daily Telegraph* to the *New Statesman*, from the *Daily Mirror* to the *Shepherds Bush Gazette*, in seeking out and publishing the views of the Young National Front, who, on the basis of a glimpse at the teachers' notes accompanying the film (which they had not seen), were announcing their intention of demonstrating outside the ILEA TV studios protesting at this

Reprinted from Dragon's Teeth *(Spring 1982), the magazine of the National Campaign on Racism in Childrens' Books.*

'shocking new brand of pro-race mixing brainwashing aimed at 13-16 year old schoolchildren', and calling for it to be banned. *Socialist Challenge* analysed the press reaction and concluded: 'the media certainly gave the NF an easy ride'.

Press ignorance

Quotes from the YNF were followed up by quotes from head-teachers: 'We're not using it; we prefer less controversial material'; 'It is a series typical of the TV do-gooders. But they end up doing a lot of harm'. There followed another set of headlines: 'Why Mandy's affair with her black lover may not be seen on classroom TV'. *Daily Mail* 'Schools wary of threat to picket race film' *TES* 'Schools tv sex series starts row' *Daily Telegraph* 'School head bans sex film' *Shepherds Bush Gazette* Some headteachers refused even to view *Somebody's Daughter,* giving such reasons as fear of parental anger if it were shown, or being 'just plain old-fashioned'.

The views of the film makers and their advisers were not sought, or if they were they were almost totally ignored. Noel Hardy, the Director, received an occasional mention, expressing the hope that 'by exposing the students to the emotional and social difficulties of characters with whom they can identify they will experience vicariously some of the feelings of living through the problems with which the plays are concerned' (and develop) 'a more mature awareness and understanding of the issues invooved.' That his advisers included such distinguished names as Gloria Cameron JP, Director of the London Youth Advisory Service, Maureen O'Connell, Head of Social Studies at Tulse Hill School, representatives of the Health Education Council, the Family Planning Association, the Centre of Urban Educational Studies, even the Consultant Obstetrician at Queen Charlotte's Hospital, was apparently of little significance to newspapers interested only in the race-hate copy provided by the 'politics' of the YNF.

A 'beautiful' film

Those teachers whom I have met who dared not only to view the series, but to make video copies and show and discuss them with their students are unanimous in the opinion that this was not only 'a beautiful, beautiful film' (FE lecturer in an Inner London multi-racial college), but the most effective life and social skills tool ever produced, and just as essential to the lives of adolescents (and their

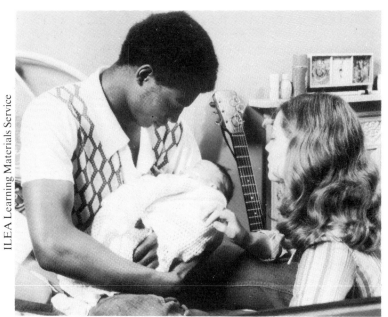

ILEA Learning Materials Service

Elvis Payne and June Page in Somebody's Daughter

parents) in 1982 as it was in 1978. Those who are fortunate enough to have their own copies tell me that it is in constant use, and not exclusively in the social studies department.

Everything my teacher friends had told me about *Somebody's Daughter* was confirmed at the press showing I attended at the ICA, when all five episodes were shown in one programme. The story of Mandy, a hairdresser's apprentice, and Winston, a HND student, who meet at FE college, fall in love and have an unplanned baby, is told with total honesty and exquisite feeling, confronting all the problems attendant upon teenage pre-marital sex, unwanted pregnancy, parental attitudes, housing, employment and the emotional stresses of single parenthood.

The question of race is courageously tackled. As the Director says in his introduction to the teacher's notes: 'Adolescent sexual mores in themselves constitute a sufficiently sensitive area: the multi-racial dimension makes it doubly so. No teacher should attempt to deal with the issue of race with young paople unless he/she has a clear understanding of the racial situation in Britain today, its historical roots, and has already a close relationship with the students involved.'

The teacher's notes for *Somebody's Daughter* provide excellent guidlines for discussion of the issues arising in each programme: from contraception to mugging, from 'the role of the father in pre-natal classes' to migration, from abortion to day nurseries. There are appendices on such things as religious attitudes in different cultures, the new race relations law, assessing children's books for a multi-ethnic society, western Europe's migrant workers, and finally a bibliography which ranges from black African novels to Diak's 'Speaking and Reading: how a child learns these skills'. And in the section dealing with mugging there is a note on the use and abuse of statistics which is more pertinent than ever in 1982!

Somebody's Daughter is more than just a brilliant educational resource. It is, as my friend the FE lecturer described it, a truly beautiful film, directed and acted with a passionate conviction that involves the audience totally with the pains and the joys of being young and in love, and living in a multi-racial society. It is a film for all ages and all races and deserves a far wider distribution than it is at present receiving. Concord films tell me that considering the importance and the wide varieties of issues which it treats they would expect it to be more frequently ordered.

Do memories of the press manhandling of the preview in 1978 still linger on? Or is this vital multi-ethnic educational resource to be a victim once again, this time of government economic policies? The ILEA find it uneconomic any longer to hire or sell video cassettes of *Somebody's Daughter*. The sole source is now Concord Films from whom you can hire the five 25 minute black and white episodes on 16mm film at £7.50 each plus VAT and carriage. Afford it if you possibly can. And why not do as we have done and write to Channel 4 suggesting that they repair the damage done by the media in the past and emulate the Dutch by showing it nationally on TV?

Making the 'Connection': Black access and local radio in Liverpool

Alex Bennett, Lynda Syed, Derek Murray

This is an edited version of a report on the Radio City community programme 'Connection', by its three presenters, Alex Bennett, Lynda Syed and Derek Murray. The programme has been running since September 1979 and faces some of the same problems as 'Black Londoners', detailed elsewhere.

The 'Connection' programme, a community/minority programme, began in September 1979, and was broadcast from 6-7pm on a Sunday evening on Radio City. Initially, it had been suggested that the programme should run for around 8-12 weeks, but this was extended more than once, and the first 'Connection' series did not end until June 1980.

The general concept was that the programme should be a black magazine programme, presenting issues which concerned black people, ranging from the local Caribbean Carnival to the Immigration Act. However, this concept was later reshaped and took the form of an inner city magazine programme, presenting *a local black perspective* on a much wider range of issues.

This reshaping came about through our contact with groups such as the Anti-Ring Road Campaign, whose objective obviously affected both black and white people in the inner city, and through the fact that many members of our potential audience were black people concerned with general community issues and white people concerned with race. Also, there are many issues which may, at first, not appear to be specifically 'Black Issues', but when viewed from a black perspective, take on a whole new aspect. This is particularly true of the section of the programme concerned with a review of the week's press reports. Another, although possibly secondary aim of the programme, was to offer the opportunity of access to experience and techniques of media presentation to a section of the community, (i.e. black people) which is under-represented in the field of local media, as in so many fields.

Finally, it had to be borne in mind that the 'City image' must play a large part in the structuring of the programme format and in the presentation. This meant, essentially, that the programme would have a strong music element and be presented by people whose personal style was not too far removed from the expectations of the Radio City audience.

The beginnings

From the community point of view, the spark for the 'Connection' programme came about, ironically, during the 1979 General Election, when John Tyndall, then chairperson of the National Front, paid a visit to Liverpool. His visit was covered somewhat eagerly by the local media, one aspect of this being an interview with him, which was broadcast as an 'on the hour every hour' scoop by Radio City. Anti-racist groups in Liverpool felt that this type of non-critical coverage was detrimental to race relations generally, and insulting to the city's black population.

Accordingly, members of one group, the Merseyside Anti-Racialist Alliance, approached the programme controller at Radio City to both make a complaint about the coverage given to the National Front's racist doctrines, and to negotiate possible airspace for the black community, according to the terms of the franchise. An agreement was reached whereby the complainants were to gather together a group of people with community involvement and contacts, to discuss ideas for a programme which would suit the purposes of both the community and the radio station, in that they could present essentially black/community issues in a reasonably 'professional' manner.

With the initial discussions concluded, the problem seemed to be to find a suitable person to present the programme. It fell to Alex Bennett to find this person. After several trials, it became evident to Alex that what was needed was a team approach. And so a team of three was formed. Alex himself, Lynda Syed and Derek Murray. Each was chosen for their abilities in specific roles: Alex had previous experience in broadcasting, Lynda was seen as the researcher and Derek provided the musical knowledge and necessary ability to chat on air. But the background that we had in common was probably more crucial to the later development of the team.

We are second generation British-born blacks. We were involved in some level of community work in Liverpool, and we had worked, and were still working on various other projects which required an exacting degree of cooperation. We are all in our mid twenties. In June 1979 we began to hold regular, often night long meetings, in order to plan a pilot tape, which was to be recorded in the Radio City studios, and which was designed to test both our potential as broadcasters and our ability to produce ideas and present them on radio.

Eventually, we produced a script for an hour long pilot tape, and this was duly recorded in City's studio, with only the three of us and one engineer. The tape was left for the programme controller. After a time, we were told that a new producer was to be employed by Radio City and that the production of 'Connection' would be a part of his work.

The format

The basic programme format consisted of approximately 50/50 speech and music, and was along these lines:
— hello and welcome
— menu
— what's on (local band spot)
— sport (the results and progress of two local football teams that 'Connection' adopted, and later the local basketball team)
— press connection (a review of the week's press reports on local and black issues)
— a 'soft' news item (such as the review of a play or a film, whose subject matter was relevant to the programme, or news of a local community group – this item usually involved an interview)
— an extended feature (a more in depth look at e.g. the new nationality proposals, or the closure of Eric's music club and the reaction of the local community to these types of issue – we accomplished this using a variety of techniques including prose, interviews, press comments and some music)

Most speech items were followed by music, preferably with a relevant theme. The format was flexible and the order could be changed.

It only became possible to deal with the likes of the Bristol riots once we had become at least competent in our use of radio techniques. One-to-one interviews were always our mainstay. We learned to do them on Uher tape-recorders in the backs of cars, in studio with an engineer and eventually in a studio on our own. We learned to edit, to work from a prepared script and to ad lib into a prepared script. As our proficiency grew in these areas, so did our confidence, so that we felt able to approach nationally known

Making the Connection: Alex Bennett, Linda Syed and Derek Murray

figures and indeed even took to ringing them at home to record interviews on relevant topics: for example, the Liverpool rugby player Mike Slemen, on the British Lions tour of South Africa.

The influence of our producer was very significant in the early stages, as he was the person we relied on for technique and guidance. He clearly saw the advantages of the cultural material readily available to us and the difficulties in presenting social/political issues. Also, we had yet to learn to identify the latter, and his being new to Liverpool meant that he could not do it for us. In fact it was the programme controller, David Maker, who helped us to begin identifying the social/political issues, and it was with his encouragement that we did so.

Within the guidelines of what we understood to be acceptable to the station and to the IBA, we began to get down to the nitty gritty of at least some of the issues. Immigration and police/community relations were two of these. In the case of immigration, we found it possible to be very critical and even to adopt a position. This was in contrast to the reaction of the police when we took what we considered to be a critical but fair view of the police complaints procedure.

Whilst the programme itself was an experiment in one form of community access, we ourselves on two occasions tried another form. What we did was to offer the resources and the skills that we had collectively acquired, along with one week's airtime, to a specific group of people, to make a programme.

By far the more successful was the collaboration with the Rastafarians. Although it took several weeks to produce, the end result was a kaleidescope of Rastafarian philosophy and culture. It contained music, poetry and speech. The high spots of the project were the two DJ 'toasting' sessions which we held in studio three, probably the first toasting to be heard on radio in this country ('toasting' is a form of DJ ad lib singing, heard at reggae discos).

The Chinese Connection was a different story. The original idea had been to present a 'Chinese New Year Special', with taped inserts of poetry, music and drama. Due to a lack of planning and time on both our part and that of the Chinese participants, we ended up with a programme which, whilst having a basic predetermined structure, was little more than a dialogue between Chinese community worker Brian Wang, and Derek. This was interspersed with Chinese music. Although the finished product was interesting and certainly of broadcastable standard, it was nevertheless a good idea that did not achieve its fullest potential.

The problems

Undoubtedly, the single largest problem in terms of resources was a place to work. Because of the nature of the structure that developed within our team, Friday became the day on which tapes were edited and scripts were written. All too often we simply could not find a desk to work at. This meant that we would often spend a whole day moving from one person's desk to another. This not only destroyed our concentration, but also resulted in tapes and pages of script being frequently lost or misplaced. It also meant that we inevitably got 'in the hair' of others who were trying to work. Obtaining access to editing facilities was a similar problem, but one which we shared with others from the Programmes department. This problem was partially solved by the reopening of studio two.

The issue of acceptance by station staff was of some concern to both ourselves and to David Maker. This can be viewed in terms of both professional and personal acceptance. There we were, a group of amateur broadcasters with no more than a few hours broadcasting experience between us, trying to produce a programme of an acceptable standard. What was expected of us by the engineers was not known. It was perhaps no wonder that their initial reaction tended to be one of dismay, frustration and even irritation. In time, the nature of the programme unfolded and people became used to working with us 'by ear', these kinds of problems were largely overcome and indeed we established a very good relationship with two or three of the engineers.

The problem of acceptance by the newsroom was more easily overcome. As we developed the social/political content of the programme, we came to have more and more reason to collaborate with them. The question of the acceptance of the team on a personal level was problematic initially. This was due on our part to a degree of suspicion of 'media people', and on their part to some oversensitivity towards the presence of an all-black group within the station. This diminished over a period of time.

Community perspectives

When the 'Connection' team was first formed, it had an uncomplicated, and to say the least, naive, approach to 'community broadcasting'. The initial response and reaction within the community, in which we live and work, was encouraging. Everyone had something to say on a variety of subjects concerning the community at large, and people were eager for an opportunity to express these views on the radio. This was short lived.

Inevitably, people began to see members of the team as unapproachable, tainted by the 'glamour' of being on the radio. It was difficult at times, during the first couple of months, to maintain any credibility with the community. This was only to be achieved through our continuing work as community workers, and our continuing involvement with non 'Connection' issues.

Feedback

Feedback on the programme has always been difficult to obtain directly. Most of the comments and criticisms have come from casual conversation and as items on the agenda at meetings. We attempted to open further channels of two-way communication with our audience. We suggested that listeners write in, and over a period of time plugged the programme's name and address regularly. We invited comment on specific issues, ran competitions and attempted an off-air phone-in session after the programme.

This latter idea ran for approximately two months, with varying degrees of response. On a number of occasions, listeners 'phoned-in' about specific items, either asking for further information; for example where and when a particular band was playing, or to comment, not always favourably, on issues such as squatters' rights. The net response of all these attempts at obtaining feedback was minimal and when measuring it against the extra burden of work and time it imposed, the team decided that it wasn't worth it.

Conclusions

The majority of the problems that we encountered have their common cause in the fact that none of the team was a professional broadcaster, or was employed by Radio City. This problem could not be solved simply by hiring someone to work on the programme. Immediately someone was employed, they would be taken from the realms of the community and community work, and the essential degree of liaison would be lost. The only reasonable way for solving such difficulties would be if a full time member of staff was made available as a reference point for the team, the only prerequisite being that they themselves were *committed* to the whole concept of the programme. Their main job in relation to the programme would be to ensure the availability of facilities and to liase between the team and other members of staff.

The second point relates much more specifically to the question of race and racial bias. On several occasions, during discussions on the presentation of a particular item, the question of bias, and biased reporting arose.

One example of, albeit unconscious, white bias, occurs regularly in police descriptions of wanted people; the adjectives 'black' or 'coloured' were used, but never 'white'. This has two consequences. Firstly it manifests an acceptance of white as being the norm, whereas for many of us it is not, and secondly, the audience begin to link those adjectives with 'criminal' automatically.

Whilst appreciating the need for a radio-station to make politically unbiased reports, it is a point of debate as to how far a programme like 'Connection' should be permitted some 'biased' reporting when the issue concerns race. After all the majority of journalistic reports are white reports. This is made more obvious in that there are still no black journalists working at Radio City − in fact there are no black employees there at all.

Part 2   The colonial view

The media and Zimbabwe
Richard Carver

The first thing to say about British reporting of Africa is that there is
not very much of it. The media suffer from a 'coup-war-famine
syndrome' — most African countries will hardly get a mention until
their president is put in front of a firing squad. Who in Britain was
able to follow political developments in The Gambia before last
summer's attempted coup? Then suddenly the papers were full of it,
complete with stranded white holidaymakers and a daring SAS
rescue. Or, to go back a bit further, who knew much abour Zaire
until the Shaba revolt in 1978 when a number of foreign mine-
workers were killed? and even then the British newspaper reader
would never have learned that the majority of foreign workers
affected were not white Europeans but Africans from neighbouring
countries.

   In some respects Zimbabwe is an exception, if only because it
has so many column inches devoted to it. But in other respects
Zimbabwe shows only too well the British media's approach to
Africa. Take the question of atrocities. When 12 Pentecostal missionaries were killed in the closing years of the liberation struggle,
allegedly by nationalist guerillas, the story was front-page news in
every British paper. The *Daily Mail* devoted four pages and an
editorial to it; the *Express* and the *Mirror* two pages each; and the
Sun one and a half pages. Just a month earlier Rhodesian forces had
killed 100 African civilians — the biggest atrocity of the war so far.
The *Express* and the *Mail* each gave it a single sentence; the *Mirror*
and the *Sun* did not report the incident at all.

   As a postscript, these same papers were surprisingly unforth-
coming when a group of British and American lawyers interviewed
a man who claimed to have taken part in the killing of the Pentecostal missionaries. He was not, as had been believed, a nationalist
guerilla but an undercover member of the Rhodesian army.

* *Richard Carver is an associate editor of* Africa Now. *He has visited
Zimbabwe since independence as a freelance journalist.*

All this will be familiar to anyone who followed the Zimbab-wean war in the British press. There was little sense that the Rhodesian government was an international outlaw, the target of United Nations sanctions and theoretically in rebellion against the British Crown. The impression was of decent white people with a similar way of life to our own under threat from bands of black savages. Since the British press cannot believe that Africans could ever act on their own behalf, there was the additional assumption that the black hordes were the advance columns of Moscow or Peking.

Language of racism

All this was reflected in the language used. White deaths were 'massacres', with overtones of primitive savagery; black deaths were 'raids' or 'hot pursuit missions', with overtones of clinical necessity. Guerillas were generally referred to as 'terrorists'. Questioned on this, the BBC said that 'terrorist' was only used to describe those who had committed acts of terror like 'killing of unarmed civilians, kidnapping children'. Yet there is no recorded instance of the term being applied to the Rhodesian regime. Indeed, the BBC was so in tune with Rhodesian government thinking that *Panorama* once described blacks working for Ian Smith's regime as 'loyal Africans' − rebellion against the Crown had presumably been forgotten.

More subtle were contortions of the *Times* in its coverage of the killing of 11 blacks by police in Salisbury in 1975. The paper first used the phrase 'Rioting blacks shot dead by police' − but by the next day the police have slipped out of the story: 'Sunday's riots in which 13 Africans were killed'. The editorial on the same day refers to 'rioting and sad loss of life', omitting all mention of who died, how, and who did it. With reference to an old standby, 'tribalism', the *Times* managed to create the impression that divisions in the nationalist movement were the cause of death.

The use of the well-worn cliché 'tribalism' is a prominent feature of journalistic coverage of Africa. One might ask what a tribe is. Every single ethnic group in Africa is referred to as a tribe regard-less of the nature of its social development. What is it that makes 3 million Welsh a people and just as many Baganda a tribe?; a few hundred thousand Icelanders a people and about 5 million Shona a tribe? As for tribes fighting each other, differences that existed between ethnic groups have been fully exploited by the British since colonial days. Today, African politicians use the differences as well.

Uneven development between regions, and thus between ethnic groups, are fully exploited to build alliances and create political support. But such an *historical* explanation is rarely, if ever, given.

News management

One reason why this sort of thing was able to pass for objective reporting in Zimbabwe is that for a long time the news was produced by a very small number of people. The most notorious case was exposed by the *New Statesman* in 1978. It revealed that Henry Miller of the *Guardian*, Peter Newman of the *Daily Mail* and Brian Henry of the *Daily Telegraph* were one and the same person: Ian Mills, the BBC correspondent. The prolific Mr Mills (still in Salisbury, by the way) has also produced material for Reuters, UPI, Agence France Presse and Newsweek.

But the problem went deeper than that. For journalists based inside the country information about the war came from a single source: the government. Department of Information handouts, Defence Ministry briefings and trips in army helicopters – that is how the news from Zimbabwe was made. To a certain extent journalists had to operate within these constraints. The legal machinery of censorship was powerful. Those who defied it were liable to end up like the *Guardian*'s Peter Niesewand – first jailed, then thrown out of the country.

However, British papers and their correspondents were not utterly powerless. One would have thought it would be standard practice in a war to assign correspondents to both sides. Yet, to the best of my knowledge, not one single Western newspaper or broadcasting network ever had a correspondent permanently attached to either of the guerilla armies. It is significant that in 1976, when he appeared at the Geneva settlement talks, Robert Mugabe was virtually unknown outside Zimbabwe. Yet he was the leader of the most effective wing of the liberation movement. When it came to the pre-independence election campaign of 1980 it is hardly surprising that the British and most outside observers so underestimated Mugabe's prospects. They made the cardinal mistake of believing their own propaganda.

By and large, the journalists based inside Zimbabwe during the war were not the victims of censorship but shared the outlook of the Rhodesian authorities. The reasons are not hard to find. The foreign correspondents were nearly all white. They shared the opulent lifestyle of most white Rhodesians; it is hard to write sympathetically about the aspirations of the black population when you have black servants to wait on table, tend the garden and clean the swimming pool.

Journalists hardly strayed outside Salisbury. A major source of information, apart from official handouts, was the gossip at the Quill Club at the Ambassadors Hotel. Over the years there have been exceptions to this dishonourable tradition, but not many.

Independence and the election campaign which preceded it were something of a hiatus in the quiet life enjoyed by correspondents in Salisbury. Their privacy was invaded by hundreds of outside journalists; in some cases they were even obliged to get out of town and take a closer look at the country that they had been writing about all those years. All were utterly fazed when Mugabe's ZANU(PF) won the election. Not only had they predicted the exact opposite; they also found that their long-established contacts with the Rhodesian political and military establishment were useless. There was a new lot in power and the journalists had hardly even set eyes on them before.

Gossip at tennis parties

What is remarkable is how things have returned to 'normal' over the past two years. Salisbury society is much the same as it has always been. The rich way of life and the black servants are still there. So is the Quill Club. The old Rhodesian politicians are in opposition but many of the civil servants are still in their jobs, providing a good source of gossip at barbecues and tennis parties.

Correspondents are still reluctant to set foot outside the city, though now they don't have the excuse that there is a war on. They have this in common with foreign journalists in most Third World countries. It is no surprise that the aspirations of the rural people who make up the bulk of the world's population go largely unreported. Foreign correspondents can only report on the land resettlement programme in Zimbabwe from the viewpoint of a white farmer or the government and civil service. They cannot put themselves in the position of an African peasant because that is quite outside their experience.

A new fund of information has become available since Zimbabwe became internationally recognised: the 'diplomatic source'. This phrase, which is liberally scattered over the foreign pages of the British press, is a sign that one is reading the opinions of the British government or its Western allies. The 'diplomatic source' approached by a correspondent in Salisbury is unlikely to be the North Korean military attaché. More likely it will be someone at the

British High Commission.

At the same time as they reflect British diplomatic thinking, journalists are likely to be in tune with British business interests as well. White society in Zimbabwe is small and closed. The representatives of British companies will be well known to journalists. And the British stake in Zimbabwean industry reads like a roll call of British firms. In some cases, of course, the companies which dominate the Zimbabwean economy have their own press interests – Lonrho, for example, which has mining and manufacturing companies in Zimbabwe and also owns the *Observer*. Small wonder that the Zimbabwean government's economic reforms such as the minimum wage legislation or its plans for a minerals marketing agency are reported almost exclusively from the point of view of foreign companies.

It might seem surprising at first sight that British press coverage since independence has been so sympathetic to the Mugabe government. Yet, as the *Sunday Times* commented after ZANU (PF)'s election victory, it has become something of a tradition in former British colonies that the Marxist ogre who leads the struggle for independence becomes transformed into the very model of a moderate Christian statesman. So it has been with Mugabe. This is not unconnected with his respect for white business and property.

Old habits die hard

It is easy to criticise Mugabe's government for the slow pace of reform and many blacks are increasingly dissatisfied with its progress. But in its defence it must be said that there are many and complex pressures on it from both inside and outside the country. In contrast, the British journalists generally live in a one-dimensional world in which the sole yardstick is how far Mugabe has managed to defer to white interests. For that reason the Zimbabwean government has tended to have a fairly good press. There is an inbuilt bias towards the status quo and that has been reinforced by all those years of rewriting government press handouts – old habits die hard.

Yet the irony is that while the British press has praised Mugabe for propitiating white interests, many of his government's more positive achievements have gone unnoted. One small example: when I was in Zimbabwe recently for a British paper I visited a ZANU-organised project to bring health care to remote rural areas. When I approached that paper's Salisbury correspondent he vetoed the story on the grounds that the subject was 'pretty boring'.

There is no improvement in sight. What is most frightening is the complacency and reluctance to change old ways. Another example from my own experience: when fighting broke out between the two guerilla armies in Bulawayo in November 1980, I was in the country and quickly visited the area. So did a number of European correspondents, though the British were thin on the ground. The Salisbury correspondent of my London paper was one of those who stayed away. This was important because the official accounts reaching Salisbury contained a number of factual inaccuracies. Most seriously, a look at the poor conditions in the camps soon revealed the cause of the guerillas' frustration. I phoned my man in Salisbury with the story. He was not interested. He filed his own account which was indistinguishable from those of his colleagues. Like them he put the incident down to 'tribal' rivalries. The main source for his story was quoted as 'British military advisers'.

Idi Amin: changing stereotypes in the British press

Bipin Patel

*When it comes to coverage of Africa, the British media deals princi-
pally in a series of imperialist stereotypes, which often obscure
complex political and social processes. Here Bipin Patel analyses
how the British press ran the whole gamut of stereotypes in their
depiction of Uganda's former president, Idi Amin − from pro-
British 'good guy', to irrational 'madman', to ruthless tyrant − and
how these simplisms hid a far more subtle reality.*

General Idi Amin came to power in a coup overthrowing Milton
Obote who had ruled Uganda since independence from Britain in
1962. During his eight years in power Amin was hardly ever out of
the media, his burly frame roaring away at the latest embarrassment
suffered by the British or the Americans or Julius Nyerere. There
was the big, stupid, black dictator, fawned on by his people, jump-
ing into the swimming pool, or about to acquire another wife.

And that's how he will probably be remembered best − a good
joke rather than the sinister dictator that he was. Fleet Street found
he made good copy; one day proclaiming himself King of Scotland,
the next telling Nyerere he would marry him if only Nyerere was a
woman and had no grey hair. He gave advice to Richard Nixon
about how to deal with Watergate and threatened to gatecrash the
Silver Jubilee party. Comedians had to include an Amin joke in
their repertoire along with Irish mother-in-laws. The humorist Alan
Coren made a few bob writing speeches in *Punch* purporting to be
made by the General.

The Times showed how important he was when, following
reports of counter-coups in Uganda, it was reported that Robson
Books, who were about to publish a collection of Coren's pieces,
'felt it would be inappropriate to publish the book if Amin were to
die in the meantime, so they took out insurance against that eventu-
ality'. *The Times* continued, 'They were offered odds of 120 to one
− £3,000 worth of insurance for a premium − and for a while at the
weekend it looked as though that was generous. But Robson are

glad Amin has survived, because they think the book will do well'.

During his reign of terror Amin was not only responsible for the murder of hundreds of thousands of people but also for reducing the once buoyant economy to a shadow of its former self. Yet the image we have of Amin is of a jovial buffoon and this image is directly attributable to the way the media characterised him in their earlier reports. This reporting began by portraying Amin as a strong and responsible leader but achieved a remarkable turnaround over the first couple of years of his rule, to finish with the 'mad clown' image we have today — this closely reflected the Foreign Office view. Although Amin did not actually carry out his coup until 1971, his influence dates back from the sixties.

Milton Obote became Prime Minister when the country gained independence from Britain in 1962. He soon became embroiled in a dispute with the Head of State, the Kabaka of Buganda. In 1966 Obote suspended the constitution, abolished the Bugandastate and the other monarchies, and assumed all power with the help of his army chief General Idi Amin. He proclaimed himself Head of State the following April, banned political parties and ordered arbitrary arrests. Not surprisingly, this did not make him popular. In 1969 he announced a 'Move to the Left' and the 'Common Man's charter'. The main function of the move was to nationalise the import-export trade and take a 60 per cent ownership in manufacturing industries. As the majority of the firms were British, Obote was not a popular man in Whitehall. To add to his sins, Obote, like Nyerere and Kaunda, was inclined to side with Biafra against Nigeria and the British oil companies. And, crime upon crimes, he, with Nyerere and Kaunda, was very vocal in his opposition to British arms sales to South Africa.

From the memoirs of Rolf Steiner, the German mercenary, we learn that a British plot to overthrow Obote and to replace him by Amin had begun in 1969, under a Labour government. A recent book *CIA in Africa* (Zed Press), actually names the British intelligence man in Kampala who masterminded the scheme. Lord George-Brown then in the Wilson cabinet hinted at the plot to overthrow Obote. The *Daily Star*'s 'Voice of Authority', writing after the fall of Idi Amin, explained why he couldn't wholly suppress a somewhat wry smile at Britain's early recognition of the post-Amin regime. The good Lord wrote, 'For I recalled that we occupied exactly the same position when Amin ousted Obote during the Commonwealth Prime Minister's gathering at Singapore in 1971'.

'Without giving away Cabinet secrets, I can reveal that Obote had given Harold Wilson a very rough ride at that and some

*Idi Amin: two media images
amiable at his wedding,
and later, the paranoid
dictator*

Keystone

previous meetings [Ted Heath was at Singapore not Wilson, but we
will let that pass] and was decidely unpopular in that quarter. Some
top Army brass told us what a first-class fellow Amin had been as a
Sergeant in the KARs (King's African Rifles). So in we went, first
with recognition'. (*The Star,* April 20 1979)

Press prefers Amin

Once Amin's coup came, Obote was not a popular man in Britain.
When the Commonwealth Heads of States met in Singapore in
January 1971, on the eve of the coup, *The Times* led the other
papers in scolding Obote and Nyerere because of their irresponsible
and extremist complaints about British arms sales to South Africa.
The Daily Express had a prophetic cartoon of Ted Heath at Singapore, pushing Obote off his yacht. The day after the coup, Tom
Stacey in the *London Evening News* reported that Obote had been
'frightening foreign investors'. He continued, 'Of the three refrac-
tory African leaders, he (Obote) was becoming the nastiest towards
Britain. At the UN, his representatives have lately led the field in
insolence and distortion of facts towards Britain and the West in
general'. Thank God he is out. But who is this new Army chap? Is
he good for Britain?

The Daily Express of January 26 1971 soothed the way. 'Military men are trained to act; not for them the posturing of Obotes of Kaundas who prefer the glory of the international platform rather than the dull but necessary task of running a smooth administration'. Tom Stacey had the following to say: 'General Amin will be good for Britain. He is a big, bluff, popular man whom everybody knows as "Idi" (pronounced Eady). Although he has not had the sophisticated training of the younger Ugandan officers – he came up through the ranks and proved himself as a sergeant and sergeant-major – he has plenty of ability'.

The heavies weren't far behind. Following Foreign Office briefings, the Diplomatic Correspondent of *The Times* reasoned '... (one can) not be able to govern long unless they can enlist the loyalty of the civil servants... and General Amin's qualifications of natural leadership makes that a practical possibility'. *The Telegraph*'s Diplomatic Staff reported: 'There is a feeling in Whitehall that General Amin will call for early elections and hand over the administration of the country to civilians. He clearly realises, it is thought, that he is personally incapable of running a country, but is determined that the next elections should be conducted on high-principled democratic lines'.

An aspect of reporting of the Third World is the weight the media put on the conditions and reactions of the white kith and kin in the country concerned. They inevitably ask a white person to size up the situation. In Uganda they asked Mrs Joyce Heckman who was Dr Obote's private secretary. She had now been reassured about the future of her job by Uganda's new Head of State. *The Times* of January 30 quoted her as saying 'I met the Major General very briefly, as he was going into a meeting with the former ministers'. She said that Amin was 'very pleasant, extremely friendly and very polite'. She was not quite certain about her future but said that hitherto she had been treated 'very well indeed, and not troubled in any way'.

Of course Idi Amin was lapping it all up and responding in the right way. *The Guardian*'s John Fairhall reported on January 27 that 'The exuberant happiness of people in Kampala and other Ugandan towns is not being pushed to the point of destroying Obote momentoes. A high medallion of Obote in the city centre still stands. General Amin explained that it was part of Uganda's history. 'I am not an ambitious man', he added. He praised Britain for giving Uganda a sound administration before independence. He wanted good relations with Britain – 'with all the countries'.

The best of British luck

Another theme always in the background when reporting Africa is that of a savage, primitive continent – a theme that implicitly justified colonial rule. Therefore even today these blacks still need our advice on how to run the show. Take, for example, Ian Colvin writing in *The Daily Telegraph*, January 29 1971. 'The example of Obote has shown how near the precipice some prominent Africans stand. These leaders need stability, aid, advice and industrial progress'. This 'advice' included Israeli assistance to General Amin in the coup d'etat. Colvin continued, 'It would be correct to say that Israeli military advisers outnumber and far outweigh those of other nations, and to those General Amin has turned for advice and sometimes protection during the past five uncertain years'.

However, in Colvin's mind, the advice had to be the right type. Concluding a detailed piece describing the conditions in Kampala, headlined 'Good Luck to Gen. Amin', Colvin wrote in *The Telegraph* (17.2.71): 'I wish him the best of British luck. I hope he may also not be inflicted with those busybody white advisers from London who fly around promoting discord in the Commonwealth'.

But journalists didn't offer a complete picture of Amin. Idi Amin had joined the King's African Rifles in 1946. In the 1950s as a Corporal, he led a brutal campaign against the Mau Mau (Kenya Land and Freedom Army) who were fighting the British in Kenya. Soon after, he was sent to disarm the Karamojo people in the north-east of the country, who were involved in cattle rustling. Amin made the warriors stand there with their penises on the tables and threatened to cut them off unless they told him where their spears and shields were hidden. The Karamojo warriors told Amin where the weapons were.

Later, the Turkhana people in the north-west of Kenya faced his platoon on a similar mission. The platoon tortured, murdered and dumped the Turkhana in shallow graves. This latest atrocity nearly brought charges against him. However, as independence was approaching the British decided not to prosecute Amin, one of the only two African officers in the Army. Despite all their financial and personnel resources, with all their sources and their observers, Fleet Street did not report this. After all why spoil what until then had been a perfect story with no complications?

Even when reports of killings started filtering out via Dar-es-Salaam, where Obote now resided, the media ignored them; there were honourable exceptions such as Granada's *World in Action* and David Martin writing for the *Observer* and *The Guardian*. In March 1971 *The Observer* reported nightly executions by firing squads at a

Nile bridge, after which the bodies were thrown to the crocodiles in the river. On July 4 David Martin writing for *The Guardian* reported that there had been fighting between troops and more killings. Ten days later Amin visited London, dined with the Queen and held talks with Ted Heath.

Again *The Telegraph* led the way in telling the public what a sensible, pragmatic person Amin was. In its leader of July 15 1971, it talked of Amin giving 'top priority to roads, hospitals, education and communication... S. Africa was down on the list... his request now for the purchase of equipment for the rebuilding of Uganda's defences deserves the most sympathetic consideration from every point of view'. *The Daily Mirror* of the same day proclaimed that Whitehall was happy with his rule. 'A thoroughly nice man. That was the summing up in London last night after a three-day look at President Idi Amin of Uganda'. 'They liked him on personal grounds. He looks every inch the heavyweight champion he once was. But in conversation he was as gentle as a lamb... They liked him on political grounds. The sale of arms to South Africa, which so infuriated his predecessor and some other African leaders, leaves Amin unmoved. '"It is not my problem", he says', reported *The Mirror.*

Whitehall responded by sending several military and police missions to Uganda and promised a £10 million development loan. But the Gentle Giant did not want any strings attached. He wanted to spend it in his own way. He had a similar problem with the Israeli government. So the money did not come through.

Stereotype changes

Shortly afterwards the brutal expulsion of the Asian community began. He flirted with Libya's Gadafy, became a devout Muslim and, lo and behold, the petrodollars started flowing in. Soon Sir Alec Douglas-Home, the Foreign Secretary, detected his mental imbalance. Yet Amin had not changed and his regime was, if anything, less wild and menacing. *The News of the World* consulted a psychiatrist to get a verdict on the 'wild man of Uganda'. Harley Street psychiatrist, Dr Ellis Stungo, told us in *The News of the World* on September 24 1972, 'No man in politics has ever faced a task as disturbing as that which now confronts Mr Heath. He is dealing, not with a politician, but with a man who is suffering from acute manic-depressive insanity'.

The Daily Mail (October 10) had this to say: 'One of the latest theories accounting for his (Amin's) madness concerns a private pilgrimage he is said to have made to Mecca last year. Shortly after his arrival, rain fell on the holy city for the first time in more than 50 years − a sign which the Moslem Amin quickly assumed to be an indication of Divine Anointment. So, after the rain, came the troubles'. *The Sunday Mirror* of September 3 carried a front-page report on 'Chequers Crisis talks on General Amin as Heath is warned − HE'S NUTS'. 'Senior Government officials now describe Amin quite frankly as 'certifiable' and 'this madman'.

By now the knives were out. Massacres were reported, some-times exaggerated, with all the gory details. Amin was now a clown. Much fun was made of his poor English. They assumed that because the General's English was limited, so too was his grasp of affairs. The reality was different. As David Saxby wrote in *The Guardian* (April 22 1971): 'On the contrary, he has shown both skill and flair in dealing with problems facing him'. Indeed, Saxby continued, 'he is regarded by Africans as a considerable linguist. A Kakwa from the north, he was brought up at Bombo in Buganda (in the south) and speaks excellent Luganda. He also speaks a trio of northern languages in addition to his own'. Perhaps in his own way he might be seen as a innovator of a language policy in Uganda. He helped to edge the country a little closer to the rest of East Africa by giving Swahili a new and politically more significant status at the expense of English.

Every action Amin took wasn't erratic but calculated. Having come to power he immediately embarked on the expansion of his military, doubling the size of the army and acquiring sophisticated military hardware, the most advanced in Africa at that time. He paid for this by starving other sectors of the economy. For example, the allocation of public expenditure upon education fell from 30 per cent in 1970 to 8 per cent in 1977. The Asian expulsion was designed to buy the loyalty of the army officers by the redistribution of the spoils and to gain popularity. His officers also took over farms as well and forced the peasants to go back to subsistence farming. As a result, agricultural production declined. The huge rise in military imports, considerably reduced the country's capacity to manufac-ture goods and produce equipment and there were no funds for other imports. Manufacturing ground to a halt because of a short-age of skills, spare parts and essential raw materials. Soon basic commodities were virtually unobtainable in the shops. They were only for select members of the army, or could be purchased at exorbitant prices on the black market which was also largely organ-ised by army officers.

The following anecdotes from George Ivan Smith's book, *Ghosts of Kampala* (Weidenfeld & Nicholson), illustrate that his killings were by no means indiscriminate but the result of cool calculation. While opponents in the army and the civil service were brutally dealt with, when the chance of international intervention threatened Amin could show his restraint. George Ivan Smith writes, 'I learnt that their (Ugandan trade union) leaders had not been arrested in spite of the fact that they made several brave statements against the regime'. Smith was told that Amin's response to their critical speeches was to demand that they should be dismissed from office. They stood their ground. He seized their funds. Although they refrained from making further public statements, they continued their work unpaid'.

Smith asked why these men went free when thousands had been killed for lesser deeds or for nothing. He was told that Amin had been warned that action against trade union leaders would bring upon him the wrath of trade union organisations from all over the world. 'Enquiries revealed', writes Smith, 'that the local staff of international banks with branches in Uganda were rarely troubled by Amin's agents... Amin did not want to tangle himself with international pipelines in the financial world. He was doing big business with his defence expenditures, his need for foreign currency was vitally important, therefore he avoided ructions with the foreign banks'.

Paradoxically the anti-Amin reporting made him a popular man in certain black circles. Having broken with Britain, he adopted the rhetoric of neo-colonialism, imperialism and Zionism. His officials convinced him that Uganda and Africa would never be free as long as they remained economically dependent on the West. Nearly two years after the coup, Martin Walker was to write in *The Guardian*, 'when one suggests to him that economic interdependence in the developed world is now so strong that no nation is "really free", he attacks the rapacity of the West. He talks of profits taken from Uganda and told me that he threw out the Israelis because they were charging the Ugandans £150,000 a day for the enormous military and economic aid effort they were putting into the country'. Walker went on to report that black Americans kept coming and going in Uganda, most of them more or less inspired by the Black Power implications of Amin's policies.

In Africa his popularity can best be gauged by the following example: When Jomo Kenyatta died, many dignitaries were present at his funeral – among them Prince Charles and Amin. A crowd gathered outside to cheer the leaders as they left the ceremony. It was noted that the cheer for Prince Charles was not as big as that for Idi Amin Dada.

Race and the BBC

The following is a selection of revealing correspondence between Liberal peer Lord Avebury and the then Director General of the BBC, Sir Ian Trethowan, about various aspects of the BBC's coverage of domestic issues of race, and African reporting.

PARLIAMENTARY HUMAN RIGHTS COMMITTEE
To: Sir Ian Trethowan, BBC Broadcasting House
From: Lord Avebury, 30 October 1980

Dear Ian,
    Thank you for your letter of October 29.
    The BBC is very like the Government, in that it has never been known to admit that it is the slightest bit to blame for anything it does, and I am satisfied of one thing; that the people at the top of the BBC genuinely believe their organisation is perfect. Otherwise you wouldn't make a remark like '... the BBC's opposition to racism is publicly known'. What everybody does know, because they can see it with their own eyes, is that the BBC has sometimes given the air to racists, as with the notorious Open Door programme, and that it employs very few black people other than in token positions. Of course the top management can be heard to profess well-meaning attitudes, but I do not detect in your programme content generally, the vigorous campaigning policy I expect from a person or body claiming that their opposition to racism is well-known. I think you would find, if you cared to make enquiries of the CRE, that eyebrows might be slightly raised by your bold assertion.

                                                    Yours, Eric

BBC BROADCASTING HOUSE

To: The Lord Avebury, House of Lords
13 November 1980
From: the Director-General

Dear Eric,
   Thank you for your further letter, dated 30th October.
   I do not think the BBC is infallible, and I try never to defend the indefensible. The BBC does admit error and we do apologise for mistakes, but I find that controversy about programmes is seldom a matter of clear-cut rights and wrongs. I also find that critics with strong opinions are often reluctant to accept that they are capable of overstating their view.
   On employment, our policy is to appoint the best people we can find. External Services, in particular, employ people from every corner of the globe. It is true that there are relatively few black programme-makers in the Television Service, but Peter Kenyatta and Prakash Mirchandani, both working in television journalism, the former as a producer, the latter as a correspondent, indicate that colour has nothing whatever to do with appointments except that in some cases it amounts to a specialist qualification as, for example, in the Asian Unit. I should add that it is insulting to suggest that these or any other of our employees owe their positions to 'tokenism' and not to individual merit. Black people are better represented in the BBC than they are in Parliament if numbers are your concern.
   Finally, I must emphasise that it is not the role of the BBC to adopt a 'vigorous campaigning policy' against racism or anything else. Unlike the newspapers, the broadcasting authorities in this country have a constitutional obligation not to 'editorialise'. I should add that we are not without black advisers on BBC advisory councils and committees, prominent among them your colleague in the House of Lords, Lord Chitnis, who serves on the General Advisory Council and chairs the Asian Programmes Committee.

Yours, Ian

PARLIAMENTARY HUMAN RIGHTS GROUP

To: Sir Ian Trethowan, BBC Broadcasting House
From: Lord Avebury, 20 January 1981

Dear Ian,

I watched the programme on King Subhuza of Swaziland on Sunday, and was amazed to find that not a single breath of criticism was allowed to intrude. The King was presented as a benevolent and wise preserver of tradition, revered by all his people, and if I hadn't known that there was another side to the story, I should have imagined that Swaziland was a paradise of unity and concord.

In fact imprisonment without trial, illegal refoulement, and persecution of opponents have all occurred there.

The lawyer, Musa Shongwe was held for months without being charged. Edward Lyons, QC MP visited Swaziland at the end of 1979 on our behalf to plead for him and he was released in May, together with 13 other political detainees. But they found it too hard to get back to their normal lives and three of them — Kislon Shongwe, Africa Khlanga and Thomas V. Maguhula, seem to have been 'blacklisted' and were not able to get re-employment.

As to illegal refoulement, the cases I have heard of were those of Dr Ernest Twala, Samuel Zwana, Simon Ngwenya and Elvis Mazibuko, who were abducted from Maputo with the tacit support of the Mozambican authorities. In March 1980 a number of Mozambican refugees were arrested in Swaziland and returned to Mozambique (Dr Twala has been picked up in 1980, August 29, by Swazi security police in Maputo (where he had gone early in July) and was driven across the border with other prisoners. On September 10, he and two others were charged with leaving Swaziland illegally! Dr Twala got a six-month sentence. His co-accused were given the option of a fine (one was Ngwenya, the other possibly Mazibuko). He should have been released January 18 but the 'Times' of Swaziland said he would face further charges. You may like to enquire whether he is still in detention.)

Refugees from South Africa are not well treated in Swaziland. The UNHCR representative there, Mr Godfrey Sabiti, would be able to confirm that he witnessed an assault by riot police on students in Mapaka, when several were beaten senseless and others were arrested and taken to Siteki police station, as far as I know, without being arrested.

Your programme ignored these facts, nor did it explain that the King had torn up the democratic constitution and reverted to a medaeval-style autocracy in 1973, with the aid of the armed South

African political police. Mr Botha must be well pleased by the way it concentrated on the quaint ceremonies, the smiling girls (a black lady croupier in the South African-only casino – how liberal can you get!) and the beautiful scenery, and the ignored reality of a feudal Bantustan, tolerated by its racist overlord in Pretoria.

Yours, Eric

BBC BROADCASTING HOUSE

To: The Lord Avebury, Parliamentary Human Rights Group, House of Commons
19 February 1981
From: The Director-General

Dear Eric,
   Thank you for your letter of 20th January, already acknowledged, about World About Us: The Lion of Swaziland.
   I agree that the film did not enter into political issues of the kind which would certainly have emerged in a current affairs programme. I think you would agree, however, that there is a place for descriptive films about little-known places and their ways of life. One such series is World About Us.
   The Lion of Swaziland set out to portray the unique character of King Subhuza II and his relationship with his people and their traditional customs. Reaction to the programme indicates that it was successful in this aim. That is not to say that we were entirely happy with the film. It was made in unsatisfactory circumstances – the production team was denied much of the access that it had been promised.
   The World About Us *makes many of its films in Third World countries whose record in human rights leaves something to be desired. Although the* World About Us *does not usually tackle human rights issues, another production team is currently involved in a series on human rights for transmission in the autumn and a series on Third World issues for transmission early next year. But in general the* World About Us *series leaves such issues to the current affairs programmes. When its study of King Juan Carlos of Spain proved to be in a very real sense a political, as opposed to a descriptive, programme we took it out of the* World About Us *and treated it as a piece of feature journalism.*
   Yours, Ian

HOUSE OF LORDS WESTMINSTER
PRESS STATEMENT: 1981 April 1, For immediate release

Carl Gardner, convenor of the Campaign against Racism in the Media and Lord Avebury, Liberal spokesman on race relations and immigration, today met top BBC officers to discuss the presentation of news and current affairs on southern Africa. The Director General, Sir Ian Trethowan, was accompanied by the Head of News and Current Affairs, Mr Neil Francis, the head of the Africa Service, Mr George Bennett and Mr John Wilkinson, Director of Public Affairs. A number of liberation and solidarity groups were contacted but were unable to attend.

The matters raised by the deputation included:—

1. Instances of BBC denial of the scientific facts of South Africa history.
2. The overwhelmingly white source of comments on racial confrontation in southern Africa.
3. The lack of specific guidelines on reporting of the unique situation in South Africa.
4. The need to monitor programmes in order to detect possible errors and bias.
5. Protection against the misleading effects of South African propaganda.
6. The emphasis given to minor cosmetic changes in the apartheid system by the BBC.

The deputation left a paper *BBC Reportage in Southern Africa* by John C. Lawrence, author of the book, *Race Propaganda and South Africa* with the Director General, who agreed to let them have a considered reply. Copies of the paper are available from Lord Avebury.

After the meeting, Lord Avebury said: 'We were disappointed to find that the BBC has no specific guidelines on the reporting of racial confrontation in South Africa. We were reinforced in our opinion that positive action is needed to prevent bias by the BBC's recognition of the difficulty of gathering news: a country where denial of access has a specifically racial dimension'.

PARLIAMENTARY HUMAN RIGHTS GROUP

To: Sir Ian Trethowan, Director-General,
BBC Broadcasting House
1 April 1981
From: Lord Avebury

Dear Ian,
   Thank you very much for sparing us some time this morning to
discuss the question of the BBC's presentation of the news on
southern Africa. I am also very grateful to you for agreeing to
examine the paper I left with you, which as I ought to have
mentioned was written by John C. Lawrence, author of the book,
'Race, Propaganda and South Africa'.
   Somebody, I think it may have been Mr Francis, mentioned that
in the course of 65 programmes on news and current affairs, slightly
over half of them contained a comment by someone whose name
indicated that he was of African or 'coloured' origin. I wonder if you
could be kind enough to let me know what is the BBC's policy on
making transcripts available of such programmes so that if one is
interested in monitoring independently the content of news and
current affairs, one would be able to do an analysis of one's own. Of
course I realise that Members of both Houses are normally given
transcripts of individual programmes if they ask for them, but I am
thinking of the possibility of an academic making a comprehensive
study of the kind you have obviously undertaken yourselves. Would
it also be possible to let us have any note which had been prepared
about the 65 programmes mentioned as an example.

                                                Yours, Eric

BBC BROADCASTING HOUSE
To: The Lord Avebury, House of Lords
23 April 1981
From: The Director-General

Dear Eric,
Thank you for your letter of 1st April.
Our policy in regard to transcripts is to make them available wherever possible, in response to specific requests. We normally have to stipulate that transcripts so received are used for private reference purposes only since the BBC only has limited broadcasting rights in the material and the non-broadcasting rights rest with the individual authors of, or contributors to, programmes. (This stipulation would apply far more to current affairs programmes than to news bulletins and there is, of course, no copyright difficulty over contributions from members of our own staff).

We also have to impose a small charge for this service since we get many requests for it and a good deal of staff time and effort has to go into the identification and retrieval of such transcripts as are available and the special preparation of those that do not already exist.

I am afraid that we cannot respond to 'blanket' requests for all programmes or programme items on a single subject. We have too many programme outlets in television and radio for that to be possible without a substantial diversion of staff from other duties.

What this comes to, in brief, is that we will try and meet specific requests from any person who wants to make a study of our coverage of South Africa, subject to the above conditions, but must leave it to that person to advise us of exactly what he wants. This is a procedure that we have had to adopt in other cases — e.g. requests from M.P.s of a broadly similar nature.

You refer to a 'comprehensive study... you have obviously undertaken yourselves' of our South African coverage. That overstates the position. We have not felt the need to initiate such a study, but we are able sometimes to make spot checks on parts of our output and the contributors to it.

Thank you for identifying the author of the CARM paper about 'BBC reportage in Southern Africa', which we are examining with interest and — as you may not be surprised to learn — with a substantial measure of disagreement!

Yours, Ian

HOUSE OF LORDS, WESTMINSTER

To: Sir Ian Trethowan, BBC
17 August 1981
From: Lord Avebury

Dear Ian,

Thank you for your letter of August 3, about the programme chaired by Anthony Howard on the inner cities.

Certainly we can agree that a tolerant society will not be achieved without allowing 'inconvenient opinion' to be expressed, though I shouldn't have thought it was an argument you were entitled to advance at the height of the controversy over the Dimbleby lecture, and at a time when the BBC is under fire in the Guardian for its censorship of drama.

But even John Stuart Mill, whose words you come fairly close to quoting, recognised that freedom of speech had a limit, where the words uttered were such as to cause harm to other people. I would argue that the expression of racism comes into this category, as Parliament has recognised in making certain kinds of utterance − those likely to stir up racial hatred − subject to the criminal law. You would say that Webster is never allowed to break the law, and that is as far as your responsibilities go. You will not see that his appearance on *any* programme is uniquely offensive to the ethnic minorities he hates so much. Nor do you appear to recognise that his contribution hardly justifies the use of the term 'discussion', but consists largely of trying to shout down anybody who ventures to criticise the National Front.

Can you really be serious in saying that Webster has an equal right to be heard? He does get some time to air his loathsome doctrines, but this goes altogether too far. If what you say represents the official policy of the BBC, we shall have to continue this discussion in public, so that others may comment. This is indeed a far cry from the words of a former Director General, who said that it was no part of the BBC's duty to give equal treatment to racism and non-racism. I haven't the exact quotation, and would be grateful if you could supply the reference, which needs to be recalled.

If all opinions should be allowed expression in a tolerant society, can you explain why Cliff Richard was permitted to explain why he played to audiences in 'Bophutatswana', but no black South African was allowed to reply? Why did you have the reporter telling us that 'black people say…' instead of giving the people of South Africa the chance to speak for themselves?

Yours, Eric

BBC BROADCASTING HOUSE

To: The Lord Avebury, House of Lords
15 September 1981
From: The Director-General

Dear Eric,
   Thank you for your letter of 17th August.
   I am sorry that you were not satisfied with my previous reply. I can only reiterate our view that it was right to include Martin Webster in Inner Cities. *I would also like to emphasise once again that my previous letter did not justify his inclusion on grounds of balance. I believe I said, rather, that racial prejudice would not go away if it were ignored and that tolerance is more effectively defended in free debate than in a monologue.*
   You ask about Sir Hugh Greene's words on the subject. I think you are referring to a passage in 'The Conscience of the Programme Director' in which he said: 'A man who speaks in favour of racial intolerance cannot have the same rights as the man who condemns it'. That statement was, of course, made some years ago and before the passage of the Race Relations Act. Nevertheless, I can assure you that we remain opposed to racialism.
   I am sorry that I cannot go more fully into your point about Cliff Richard, as you do not say to which programme you refer. As you know, however, we do not undertake to achieve perfect imbalance within every individual programme and I hope you will accept that we do endeavour to represent the opinions of black South Africans in our general coverage of that country's affairs.

                                        Yours, Ian

Employment, training and the work of the Black Media Workers' Association

Gary Morris of the BMWA

The Black Media Workers' Association (BMWA) is an autonomous organisation that brings together people of an Afro-Caribbean, Asian and African descent. We have no affiliation with any political party or campaigning organisations, and pursue an independent line of analysis and action.

The origins of the BMWA are very much like that of any group of individuals who come to constitute a body of common interest. We were people who met socially from time to time and who gradually became aware that the problems they faced as workers, either in the independent black media, or the mainstream white media, were capable of common expression. Feelings of isolation, frustration and the resulting alienation were transformed in such a way as to become a focal rallying point for something more than supportive solidarity, subsequently to prove itself so important for sustaining the association. The Black Media Workers' Association (BMWA) was formally launched in February 1981 – in keeping with its diverse and open nature at a meeting attended by over 150 people from all walks of community life.

Black video group

The work of the BMWA might usefully be divided into two parts. One can be termed *concerns of the profession,* which range from items like improving the independent black media, through to monitoring the way the press perpetuates racism and imperialism – and taking these issues up with bodies like the media unions. The second area of our activity might aptly be termed *concerns of the black community*. In practice this has led to activities like setting up a video group, which is presently involved in making a tape on 'Black People and the NHS'. We also try to give groups involved in campaigns access to both the black independent media and the mainstream, so as to promote an important viewpoint that would otherwise go unheard.

The areas of *Training* and *Employment* are in our view very much inseparable from our commitment to the black community, in that black people expect to be able to seek and obtain employment in the media, and upon being employed, to have the same rights and conditions in their jobs as anyone else. Thus BMWA have put a lot of time and energy into trying to eliminate the racism that results in our under-representation in a whole range of jobs across the media industry – and produces an impoverishment of the media generally.

When we allege that racial discrimination is in fact taking place, we are usually confronted by one of two arguments. The first challenges our ability to make such statements at all on the grounds that we can offer no concrete proof of racial discrimination. The second argument used to rebuff our charge (and it has slight variations) maintains that suitably qualified black people do not exist, or that their work is unprofessional – and therefore they are ineligible for jobs or for promotion to a higher position. The dispute which erupted over the programme *Black Londoners* is an illustration of why BMWA attaches so much importance to the interconnected issues of employment and training.

Around the mid-70s BBC local radio introduced a slot of airtime devoted to what was called 'access' programming. The term 'access' simply meant that members of the community were invited to make programmes that reflected a community viewpoint, hitherto unrepresented. In this way *Black Londoners* came into being. The programme developed from a monthly to a weekly programme, and rapidly rose to national and international prominence. The people required to run this programme were never given adequate resources to produce it, despite its markedly advanced status in comparison with similar (and dissimilar) programmes. People who worked on the programme often acquired their training 'on the job'.

This feature of employment, resulted in two grave drawbacks. Firstly their career chances were limited because they lacked the requisite formal qualifications and training. In addition, what was being produced by black broadcasters was not often fed into mainstream programmes at peak listening hours – partly a result of the

BMWA founder member Diane Abbott and other media workers chat together at the group's conference at the Commonwealth Institute in July 1981

lack of formal training, compounded by racial chauvinism on the part of the programmers. Exceptions were made, however, for moments of national tension − for example when the body politic reeled under the frustration of disaffected black youths on the streets. These accumulating dissatisfactions led black workers on Radio London to confront the management, since they needed full control of programme-production, and considered themselves to be fully-fledged professional broadcasters. The *Black Londoners* example clearly points up why the issues of employment and training are vitally important, both in respect to career-prospects and the on-air product.

Research into employment

The task then of the BMWA has become one of responding to these criticisms, so as to leave the employer with no further excuses for not employing black people. Towards the achievement of this aim, BMWA has obtained a commitment from the NUJ, ACTT and the ABS, to ensure that research is done into the employment of black people throughout the whole media industry. This work is being undertaken with a view to the possible introduction of quotas to prevent the persistent under-representation of blacks. In response to the arguments of young black people, complaining that they had no idea how to enter the media-industry, BMWA have produced a leaflet giving instructions on where to apply for certain jobs and what types of qualifications are required. Thus we have gone some way towards firmly meeting the criticism concerning the lack of suitably-qualified job-applicants, as well as beginning to ensure that black people can be adequately trained.

Employer attention is also being directed to the publications that black people actually read and they are being encouraged to advertise in the independent black press, so that suitably qualified black people do come forward. In addition we have undertaken to sponsor a course on radio and print-journalism, in conjunction with the Polytechnic of Central London, which is due to start in the coming academic year, 1982-83. The course is particularly illustrative of the approach of the BMWA, for in it we have tried to ensure that a carbon-copy of the white journalist is not produced, by giving the course a black perspective. Training for us constitutes part of our attack on the white bias so firmly entrenched in the mainstream media industry.

Build black media

As well as attacking the mainstream white media, BMWA are also concerned to strengthen the independent black media, because it is one of the small areas of the media industry as a whole over which we exercise some effective control – and are therefore in a position to make most rapid progress. The training that is acquired in the independent black media is something that we would seek to improve, not only just from the point of view of ensuring that there is ample provision to learn from all the possible range of skills in the various media, but more so as to ensure that employment prospects are not restricted, should a black person wish to seek employment elsewhere. Our aim then is to make sure that black personnel already established in the independent black-owned media are equipped to transfer to white mainstream media or make an input into it via independent productions. BMWA intend to run a series of workshops, at weekends, in various aspects of the media-industry, so as to facilitate this process. The status of people who acquire skills in this way is still a matter we have to pursue with the trade unions and employers.

Race, press freedom and the right of reply

Aidan White

Media freedom is, or at least it should be, the cornerstone of any democracy worthy of the name. It should mean a press and broadcasting system rich in conflicting opinions. It should mean high ethical standards from people who work in the trade. And it should mean the established right of people who have been unfairly represented to defend themselves without the burden of costly legal battles.

But in Britain media freedom means nothing of the sort. To Lord Goodman, who in 1975 was the chairman of the Newspaper Publishers Association – the people who run national newspapers, press freedom depended on 'the right of the man who controls the newspaper to say what he likes, no matter how perverse, absurd or cross-grained'.

Given such a precise definition it is easy to see how the notion of media freedom is mere fantasy. It is an illusion given substance by claims that editors are 'independent' and that the Press Council is a serious watchdog organisation. Neither, of course, bears much resemblance to how things really are. Editors are appointed by directors of companies looking for people to represent their interest in the editorial field and the Press Council is a largely establishment body, without any power to enforce its judgements, even if it made any which offered any challenge to the power of Lord Goodman and his friends.

But for people not fortunate enough to own their own newspaper or television station serious problems remain. How do we get our points of view fairly reported, particularly when they are not part of the commercial mainstream and, of pressing importance, how do we answer back if we are unjustly criticised?

---

* Aidan White is a former national committee member of the Campaign for Press and Broadcasting Freedom. He was a founder member of the East End News co-operative and is currently deputy women's editor of The Guardian.

Action against bias

It's a general issue, but black people have good cause to demand immediate answers to these problems. The reporting of the Deptford fire in South London when 13 people died, and the subsequent inquest, tended to play down the impact that this tragedy had on the black London community. And the sensational and racist treatment of a demonstration by predominantly black people to demand official action to find the killers clearly showed that the media is only interested in black community news in the context of violence.

This attitude reflects a general establishment perspective − as the decision of the Metropolitan police to break down crime figures on an ethnic basis indicates. Why, for instance, was there no Fleet Street newspaper which inquired as to why the figures indicating criminal responsibility were not broken down in a more relevant context, say on the basis of those in employment and those out of work?

How can the bias be challenged? In fact, it might appear that very little can be done. Very often the only answer for people who need to hit back is some form of direct action which has been a feature of the response by some trade unionists recently.

For example, ASLEF workers at King's Cross − supported very strongly by other railway workers − felt that the only way they could reply to the orchestrated attack by *The Sun* during the recent rail drivers dispute was to black all of Rupert Murdoch's newspapers from their trains, including *The Times* and *The Sunday Times*. A front page attack on railway workers that supposedly exposed wholesale skiving among workers in the industry was a typical piece of news intervention aimed at undermining the workers involved, at bringing them into public ridicule and discredit and at strengthening the management's policy of confrontation. What alternatives did the railway workers have to direct action?

They could have sent in a reader's letter. But that could have been edited if *The Sun* executives didn't like it. Nor would it receive anything like the prominence of *The Sun*'s original offending article which had sensational treatment and took up most of the front page.

They could have complained to the Press Council. But it takes months to go through the process. And anyway, even if it went the union's way − which in terms of previous Press Council findings was highly unlikely − there is no guarantee that *The Sun* would have accepted the finding, or that they would have given the finding any more prominence than is given to a reader's letter.

They could have sued for libel. This is the rich man's right of reply. The cost of libel actions is extremely high and only those with people who believe they have been libelled. And, of course, given the attitude of the courts in recent years to trades unions in disputes, there was no encouragement to go ahead, even if they had the bank balance to pay the lawyers' bills.

So the railway workers resorted to their own form of reply. Their action stirred up a predictable response from the media owners about attacks on press freedom. It was not a very satisfactory response, because in itself it led to further criticism of their action and it did not lead to ASLEF getting anything like a fair hearing in its own defence. There was very little else they could do.

Media reform

There is no reason why this should always be the case. It may well be that wholesale reorganisation of the media to give it the look of a relatively liberal-minded system of communication is a long way off, but there are serious efforts being made to bring influence to bear within the industry itself. The Campaign for Press and Broadcasting Freedom was launched almost three years ago in the wake of some of the worst journalism seen for many years – the reporting of the so-called 'Winter of Discontent' strikes by local authority workers.

The campaign sees the need for greater links between the people who work in the media and those who are victims of its excesses. What this has meant has been a continuing effort to bring together media and other workers around a common set of aims for media reform. Some 24 national trade unions are affiliated.

The need to focus attention on the problems of people who have no rights in the face of media bias led the campaign to launch its right of reply initiative. Here, through a booklet supported by the general secretaries of all the major media unions, the campaign argues for common understanding between people who work in the media and those outside so that joint pressures can be applied to ease the grip of employers on news and information. It is intellectually a powerful case: the establishment *as of right* in a liberal democracy of a process where anyone, irrespective of means and belief, can obtain fair redress when the media goes over the top at their expense. Something convenor Derek Robinson of British Leyland might have been glad of.

The Campaign for Press and Broadcasting Freedom is not able, however, to go as far in its demands as may be necessary to cure the media's knee-jerk hostility or organised labour, Left-wing ideas and organisations, ethnic minorities and feminist groups. It is a broad

THE
RIGHT
OF
REPLY

A guide for those misrepresented and
misreported in the press and other media.

With a preface by
Moss Evans, Bill Keys, John Jackson,
Owen O'Brien & Joe Wade

Campaign for Press Freedom

alliance of people and organisations of differing political and industrial opinions and has to treat a careful trail so as not to promote conflict within its own ranks.

The people who work in the media are divided themselves. The NUJ has a Code of Conduct which, over the past ten years, has been amended several times to make it as pure as the driven snow, but in terms of changing the traditional attitudes of journalists, the conduct and, indeed, the union has had as yet, only marginal influence. There is a growing industrial consciousness within the union as the actions of recent years have shown. But the recession with its inevitable consequences for job security has had the effect of whittling away at the confidence of journalists in challenging their employers' attitudes.

Ways to complain

That, however, is no excuse. Journalists who have taken it upon themselves to work in the business of free expression should, at least, be expected to stand out against unfair pressure and bias within their own business.

The NUJ Code of Conduct is, theoretically, in effect for about 80 per cent or so of all the journalists in Britain. It's hardly too much to ask that it should be implemented. The Union nationally and locally has taken on the commitment to improve standards of journalism and it's worth taking them up on the offer. There are a number of things that people can do to help the NUJ along:

1) *Complain:* If you have a complaint about how an article is written or don't believe you have been fairly dealt with and you have failed to get any satisfaction from the publication (printed or broadsheet) concerned then raise your grumble with the NUJ nationally (314 Gray's Inn Road, London WC1) *and* locally − write and demand to talk to local NUJ officials at branch or office (chapel) level;

2) *Organise:* Involve other people who can help in your complaint. Get the local trade unions at the Trades Council to take up your protest, contact printing unions or broadcasting unions nationally or locally and ask them to intervene on your behalf,

3) And, if necessary, take *direct action:* a demonstration outside or inside a journalists office has a wonderful effect in concentrating the mind on your complaint − but it's only advisable to prepare such intervention when all other efforts have failed.

In the end, of course, the problems that people who read, watch and listen to the media face can only be overcome by mounting opposition and protest to such an extent that wholesale reorganisation of the media becomes inevitable. The time is fast approaching when sweet words are not enough − journalists and everyone else in the business have got to start doing something about it.

It ain't half
a hot potato, Mum

Carl Gardner

*An account of the making of CARM's 'Open Door' TV programme,
'It Ain't Half Racist, Mum'.*

The Campaign Against Racism in the Media's *Open Door, It Ain't
Half Racist, Mum* was the 171st access offering of the six year series.
But it was the first programme to address itself critically to television itself, and to the BBC in particular. It was also the first programme made largely by people who work in and around television.
As we shall see, these two facts stretched to breaking point the
liberal veneer of the medium and its amenability to criticism.

The programme was accepted by *Open Door* early in the
summer of 1978. From the beginning they knew it was going to be a
hot potato. There was some initial hostility and suspicion on both
sides – in particular the Community Programmes Unit was initially
resistant to some of our ideas and working methods. We were told
we couldn't view material off BBC premises. We were told we
couldn't use our own editor for the programme, despite the fact that
he worked for the BBC in a freelance capacity and had his own
editing equipment. We were told that an experienced researcher in
the group couldn't gain access to the BBC library, despite being well
acquainted with it. And reasons were put forward why some of the
materials we wanted were inaccessible.

However, once we had established that we knew what we were
doing and wouldn't be fobbed off with technical/legalistic excuses
(which could have completely put off programme-makers with less
experience) the Unit began to co-operate wholeheartedly with us
and we established a fruitful working relationship.

Our main problems didn't concern the *Open Door* unit. Neither
were they technical, though these are worth mentioning. Because

* *Carl Gardner is the TV editor of* City Limits *magazine. A founder-member
of CARM, he was also co-writer and co-producer of the BBC2 'Open Door'
programme, 'It Ain't Half Racist, Mum', broadcast in March 1979. This
article is reprinted from* Time Out, *February 23, 1979.*

we had to have several racist situation comedy clips transferred to film, for editing purposes (video editing is a very long and costly process), we used up our film budget very early and therefore were driven into the studio for a substantial part of the programme, almost against our will. Secondly we had planned to use a modern Riley caption-machine, to fire worded questions and comments over the clips we would use to illustrate our argument. Very late we found that the machine was in use for another programme, on the day allocated for our studio-recording.

Unequal treatment

The big problems came when we wrote to the various department heads and producers in News, Current Affairs and Light Entertainment (commercials were ruled out due to legal complexity and cost) for permission to use clips of their programmes to substantiate our arguments about how television deals with race. We were completely open in our intentions but these requests triggered a lot of heart-searching in the Corporation corridors and in ITV. Some producers said we could look at programmes but not necessarily use them in our final programme. There were some odd refusals – and even more unexpected instances where permission was given. For example Brian Lapping on *World in Action* (Granada) refused us permission to use their documentary on the National Front, despite the fact that we wanted to use it as an example of good anti-fascist coverage! He didn't want his programme to be associated with fringe groups like ours.

On the other hand Humphrey Barclay of London Weekend gave us permission to use clips from their eminently criticisable comedy programmes, and John Dekker of the BBC gave us carte blanche with his three-part documentary series *Race*. Several producers refused permission without giving any reason – when asked for a written reply to our request, one producer at the BBC exclaimed 'Not bloody likely'. Another is reported to have said: 'We're not going to be held up as an Aunt Sally by a bunch of loony lefties!'

The reply from Roger Mills, BBC Executive producer, Documentary Department, to our request for clips from *Behind the Front* (which the NF openly applauded) was particularly interesting. 'To allow those extracts to be used would be tantamount to an admission that we made an irresponsible programme. I am certain we did not make an irresponsible programme… I hope you will understand that the integrity of our programmes is something we value highly'.

But the major struggle was over BBC and ITN news. Not unexpectedly we got the thumbs down from both, but the ensuing debate with the BBC over the decision revealed a lot about the ethos and attitudes of the Corporation's hierarchy. Refusals from both BBC and ITN were not unprecedented. When LWT's *Look Here* did a small item on media racism last summer fronted by black journalist Mike Phillips, no co-operation was forthcoming from either department. In our case ITN refused to give any reason at all for their decision, but the BBC's editor of TV news, Alan Protheroe, sent us a lengthy letter on December 4.

Access – at a price

'It is not the BBC's policy and never has been, to make news film available to any organisation whatsoever, which is beyond our editorial control... We realise that the principle conflicts with those underlying the BBC's facilitating access programmes such as *Open Door*. Accordingly your case was given the most careful consideration and the decision confirmed at the highest level in the BBC. Please be assured that we in TV News would like to do as much as possible to help you examine the coverage of racial matters in our part of the media. I understand that ways in which this might be done have been suggested to Mike Fentiman (Editor, Community Programmes) and no doubt he will be discussing these ideas with you'.

Firstly it is not true that TV News don't make film available outside their editorial control. They supply various news-film agencies with footage for national and international distribution. Many programmes inside the BBC, including *Grapevine* and even a recent *Open Door* have used such footage for illustrative purposes. And independent films like *Blacks Britannica* and *Dread, Heat and Blood* used lots of BBC News footage outside the BBC's editorial control. Protheroe's suggestion of ways to help us consisted of a proposal that he, Alan Protheroe, be interviewed on the programme. We suggest that he extends that principle to his own news coverage – when black spokespeople are regularly interviewed after critical news coverage, then we'll accord the same privilege to Mr Protheroe. 'The highest level of the BBC' referred to was the BBC's weekly Editors, News and Current Affairs meeting. By the time we received Protheroe's letter, we had already obtained a copy of the normally restricted minutes of the meeting on November 21, 1978, at which the CARM request was discussed.

The meeting was plainly split between the liberals – 'The media should be strong enough to accept that its reporting might be questioned' – and the hard-liners – 'Why should an organisation which might well accuse the staff of racism be given privileged treatment?' That latter remark was our friend Mr Protheroe again.

However we didn't let the matter rest there, but wrote to the Chairman of the BBC, Sir Michael Swann. His reply of January 16, 1979 simply repeated the earlier arguments, stressing the Corporation's apparent legal right to sit on its output and adding, 'We need to be satisfied that it will not be edited or used in a context which may distort its original meaning or relevance.

Damning evidence

Obviously TV is very touchy about the question of race. Certainly it is the area where the media in general are least amenable to critical discussion. Perhaps it has good reason, given the material we showed in the *Open Door* programme. Despite the non-cooperation of our broadcaster, we knew we had accumulated some damning evidence. Events after transmission were equally illuminating. So sensitive were the BBC to our mini-barrage of criticism, that they instructed BBC Enterprises (the Corporation's marketing arm) not to allow further sales of the programme. Even CARM itself was instructed that it could not show the programme, except to its own members for educational purposes. And access to the master video-tape for further copying was made extremely difficult. And according to the minutes of a meeting of the heads of BBC News and Current Affairs, which discussed the programme, one leading BBC executive described us as using 'the methods of Dr Goebbels'. But the crowning glory and sign that the production struck at the heart of the beast, came in June, when prior to another *Open Door* programme, the BBC broadcast an abject apology to Robin Day, Ludovic Kennedy and others, who we had lambasted, 'dissociating itself' from any suggestion that they were racist. This despite the fact that the programme had been legally checked twice, prior to transmission and after, and found watertight. Evidently TV is very good at dishing out criticism, but not too good at taking it.

It Ain't Half Racist, Mum was transmitted on BBC's *Open Door* on Thursday March 1 and Sunday March 4, 1979. It is available for hire on 16mm film or VHS, Phillips and U-Matic video-cassette, from Other Cinema Distribution, 79 Wardour Street, London W1 (01-734 8508) or Concord Films, 201 Felixstowe Road, Ipswich, Suffolk (0473 76012).

The NUJ and race: the work of the union's race relations working-party

Phil Cohen

The NUJ's Race Relations Working Party was set up in 1974 and has a current annual budget of £2700. It exists to raise with its members the issues of race reporting, bias in the media and sensitivity towards ethnic minorities and communities, as well as dealing with individual complaints that are referred to it from the public. As from the 1982 annual conference five members are elected by ADM (annual delegate meeting); two represent the national executive and others are co-opted from union branches where it is thought they will bring expertise to bear or represent a region that is not already covered. As the 1982 annual report said: 'A vast amount remains to be done. Too many members still flout the Code of Conduct, albeit unconsciously, and too many others are prepared to tolerate this unhappy state of affairs. Coverage of the activities of black people – other than in a critical context – is rare, and undoubtedly contributes to the alienation felt by many black people'.

The union's code of conduct referred to states that journalists should not 'originate material which encourages discrimination on grounds of race, colour, creed, gender or sexual orientation'. It is voluntary and not binding, although members of the union or the public can bring complaints against journalists who they feel have breached the code or inflamed racial tension in some way. Under rule 18, a union branch can consider such a complaint and if it feels there is a *prima facie* case will refer it to the national executive. The NEC may first try conciliation between the parties and/or hold a formal inquiry. It has the power to impose fines not exceeding £1000, suspend a member for not more than 12 months or expel the member from the union. An appeal structure is built in at every stage. The rules make it clear that mambers can take up complaints about media coverage on behalf of non-members – i.e. the public.

* *NUJ Race Relations Working Party member since 1979.*

Proving complaints

Few complaints are in fact ever laid, partly out of ignorance of the system, and when they are, it is often difficult to prove a breach of the code. For instance, there were several complaints against Fleet Street coverage of the march through London when black people protested about police inaction on the New Cross fire tragedy, in which 13 young black people died. The London Freelance Branch of the union made complaints which were investigated but it was difficult to precisely pinpoint which sub-editors had written particular inflammatory headlines, and the union officials at these papers refused to co-operate. Some complaints were dropped and some found not proved. This illustrates the difficulties that exist in combatting racist copy under rule. In 1982 the NUJ conference recommended some changes in the Code of Conduct and complaints system, which may begin to solve some of these problems.

The NUJ has already agreed guidelines for all members to follow when dealing with race relations subjects and when reporting right-wing racist organisations. These have also been adopted as the policy of the print unions (see Appendix).

The working party itself periodically holds meetings around the country, normally in cities where complaints have been made about race coverage. Attempts are made to speak to NUJ chapels, newspaper editors and management from local radio, and public meetings are often held to which journalists and black community groups are invited. In the last three years, such meetings have been held in Liverpool, Leicester, Bristol, and Glasgow. The public meeting in Liverpool saw a lively debate, with a *Liverpool Post* editor defending the paper's coverage of muggings in Liverpool 8, where a majority of the city's black community live, against allegations of racism.

In Leicester representatives of the Asian community said their activities were not reported by the local paper, *The Mercury*, which had no black reporters or anyone specifically covering race relations. There was a well-attended meeting in Dundee on the subject of 'Making the Most of the Media' despite DC Thompson management's refusal to accept an advertisement from NUJ members about the meeting. Public meetings have been held around the issue of poor press coverage of the Barnet trials of defendants arrested in Southall in 1979. A Southall Defence Campaign film was shown. Another took up the Brixton riots and Fleet Street reporting. The latter two attracted few journalists from national papers, underlining the apathy among them on this issue.

The working party has also helped to finance a weekend conference for black media workers in Birmingham at which 150 black people took part and which played a vital part in building up confidence of black media workers who had previously been isolated in their own newspapers, magazines and broadcasting stations.

An 'orgy' of offence

It has given financial support to the Black Media Workers Association and to other local groups producing anti-racist literature.

Occasionally the working party issues press statements on topical matters. It complained of 'a spate of racist and offensive cartoons' published in British papers during the Commonwealth Conference in Lusaka in 1981. It drew particular attention to cartoons in *The Sun, Daily Mail* and *Daily Express* 'in which such themes as savagery and cannibalism has been used freely to attack black people' and considered these were 'a denigratory depiction of black people'. It called on NUJ members in the national and local press to draw to the attention of chapels and editors what it saw as 'an orgy of offence that has passed for humorous political comment on a major issue of the day'.

In April 1980 the working party protested to Home Secretary William Whitelaw about the sacking of five commissioners of the CRE which was seen as a political move against those who were pressing for more radical action against discrimination. As the then deputy general secretary of the union Charles Harkness said: 'Events in Bristol and elsewhere have shown, we feel, a need for dynamic action on the problems of our inner cities and the question of race relations generally. In this respect the announcement on reappointment is a severe blow'.

The task of achieving equal opportunity in training and recruitment for black people seeking to become journalists is still a major one. Until employers are prepared to reach out to the black community through contacts with careers officers and schools and advertising in the black press, the numbers of black journalists will not significantly increase. The working party is co-operating with the National Council for the Training of Journalists to monitor black students who apply for training courses and is also urging the NCTJ to monitor those who finally succeed. In one survey by the NCTJ out of 141 applicants only five were black.

The issue of black employment in the media is probably the most important that the union has to tackle. The 1982 NUJ conference 'urged Industrial Councils to ensure that all claims include demands

for positive action to be taken to encourage employment of journalists belonging to ethnic minorities'. This demand will have to be
backed up with grassroots action by journalists and support for the
work of the Black Media Workers Association, so that both media
employment and media coverage fully reflect the reality of Britain's
multi-racial society.

Race on TV – switching channels?
Sue Woodford interviewed

Sue Woodford is Commissioning Editor at Channel Four for Multi-Cultural Programmes, and was formerly a Producer/Director for World in Action. She is interviewed here by Tony Freeth for CARM.

Q: Would you say something first of what you think is wrong with the media in relationship to black people?

A: Basically the problem is that the media is almost exclusively controlled by white people, and television programmes are made by white middle class men on the whole. Therefore there is no opportunity for any different perspective to come through, because all the people who are making decisions are part of nothing but a very narrow group.

What exactly do you see as the areas of the worst offenders on television – news, sit-coms, or drama?

I think they are all bad. I think the news is very bad. For example if you look at the coverage last summer, it took a very long time before you actually saw black people speaking about what was going on. And then it was the established so-called community leaders who spoke towards the end. There was not a single black reporter, reporting what was going on in Brixton, in Toxteth, in Bristol. Black journalists have to have a different view. They live in the community, they are part of the community, and they know what's going on in the community. And yet their perspective was never put forward. You didn't even see any black kids. It was at least three weeks before you got a programme, (it was *Panorama*) which actually allowed young blacks to talk for themselves about what was going on in their environment during that period. There is obviously nobody in ITV or BBC who is reporting on the network who has any relationship with black people at all, or to the black community.

So would you say that television is racist, or is that too much of a generalisation?

Well, I think that the image that you get is racist. I mean that is the natural logical conclusion of saying that television doesn't reflect the black community in any sense — there is no outlet, for their views, opinions or perspective. Television doesn't even employ black people in any numbers and certainly there are almost no black people in decision-making positions in television. The end result of that has to be that you get a racist broadcasting perspective. I am not saying that all individuals who are working in television are racist — in fact the vast majority would say that they are not. They are thoroughly good liberal people who don't discriminate against women or blacks. But if you look at the reality of the situation those groups are not part of the broadcasting system, therefore their views never get expressed. So it is perfectly reasonable to say that it is as sexist as it is racist.

You said that the majority of people would say that they are not racist, you didn't actually say that you necessarily believed they weren't?

I think it depends entirely on how you define racism. They do not make any positive attempt to allow black voices to come through — now they wouldn't say that was racist, but the end result of ignoring that situation, of not doing anything positive to change it, is that. Certainly black people feel that television is racist.

You mentioned the news, perhaps you would like to talk about other areas in terms of content?

I think comedy has to be one. I think in many ways that it is worse because more people watch it. For example, *Mind Your Language* which is very, very popular and which deals exclusively in racist stereotypes, white as well as black.

How do you think that sort of comedy actually affects people — in particular white people?

Well, it reinforces their prejudices and it makes them feel much more comfortable about being racist. It makes it more respectable — the Alf Garnett syndrome. I think what he did actually was to make extremely racist views more generally acceptable and give respectability to them.

We have looked at news, and comedy programmes. If you look at straight drama and so on, do you see any omissions there?

I'm not an expert on drama. I don't watch a lot of drama. I think that the most glaring omissions are that black playwrights are not being given an opportunity to write for television. They are not being *encouraged* to write for television. I think there again there is no positive effort to look for black writers. Drama tends to be very conservative — people who commission drama tend to go for known playwrights. I suppose the other area is that there is very little attempt made towards integrated casting.

What do you mean exactly 'integrated casting'?

the only time that black actors and actresses ever get hired is when there is an obvious stereotype – a nurse, or a doctor, or a bus conductor. Then directors will think that casting black people is all right, that we can have somebody black for that part. But there is no sense in which they get black actors and actresses to play a part because they are good actors and actresses.

Would you be in favour of a quota system?

Well, people just freak out when you mention quotas. They get terribly worried about it, so I have stopped using the word, because it seems to upset people so much. They are also illegal under the existing legislation. I really don't know what you can do if you are running a drama department. I suppose you could say we have to positively attempt to identify all good black actors and actresses in the country and we have to make sure they are taking part in production, that we are giving them work. I don't personally have any objections to quotas, but they seem to upset people so much. It is very much easier to achieve your objective without mentioning the word quotas.

What are your priorities for combatting racism on television?

I think there has to be positive action. Just to have a few more black faces on the screen is not going to change anything at all. The fundamental thing is, I think, to get more black people into the industry, at all levels of production including technical grades. And then somehow get them moving up the promotion ladder.

How do you think they should go about doing that?

I think that broadcasting organisations should be actively looking for people to hire. I have been told that the BBC are going around Universities, going around communities, going around sixth forms and actually trying to identify commited black people who have an interest in the media. And they are also trying to make sure that they bring in black people to their training courses. That is what I am told by Jocelyn Barrow, who is a governor there, that they are beginning to do that, they have actually agreed that there is a problem.

Are there any other training schemes?

There is a National Film School training initiative that has just been launched, and there is an Advisory Committee which has on it, members of all the unions plus representatives from ITV, BBC and Channel Four. At the moment there is a three month research period going on. The aim is basically to examine the training needs of the industry, with particular emphasis on equal opportunities, and to run some pilot short courses. Among those short courses one will be strictly for women, and one will be strictly for black people. At the end of the three month period, they will try and assess the long-term needs for more systematic training, and to have specific

Sue Woodford: no change in television without positive action

longer term courses in order to bring more blacks into the industry.
Are you satisfied with the unions on this question?
No, absolutely not. I mean, they are absolutely appalling. It is
totally absurd that I cannot get together here an all-black crew, I
just can't do it.
Why?
Because there aren't enough black union members. That must be

the fault of the unions.

Well, the fault of the unions and the Companies that don't actually employ them. Do you feel that the unions have actively kept black people out?

No. They haven't thought about it, it hasn't occurred to them there is a problem. I don't think there is really an active attempt to keep black people out. I have never come across that in the areas I have been working in, but what happens is just as bad, because they are excluded. It is lack of awareness of identifying the problem, and trying to find ways of doing something about it.

I believe that ACTT has now an equal opportunities officer?

Equality Officer — Sandra Horne — she is very good, but she has a massive task ahead of her!

If we could talk a little about Channel Four — could you say what your job actually is?

Commissioning Editor for multi-racial programmes. Under the Act that set up Channel Four, the channel has a specific commitment to reflect the different cultures and different communities that actually make up the country we live in. It is up to me as to how that is done. I have said all along — in fact it was a condition I made when I took the job — that we would not be talking about ghetto programming but that we would have a channel which as a whole reflected every area of a society in which fifty one per cent of the population are women, and a large proportion are not white anglo-saxon protestants. And certainly up to this point I have had no suggestion that the channel doesn't actually have a very genuine commitment to that. Over the years, I have been a huge cynic, but I really think that there is a very genuine commitment here, from Jeremy Isaacs downwards, and will be one that is carried out.

How have you actually been going about getting programmes made from a black point of view?

I have identified, I think, the fact that to make a real contribution, to achieve anything in this job, what I need to do is to try and push forward the training opportunities, and I am starting to look at that, very seriously. I'm having a big input into the National Film School training, which I hope will result in something long-term.

So where will the funding come for that?

I think we are going to have to make the ITV companies pay and to make the BBC pay something, convince our independent producers that it is in their interests to broaden the range of people they employ and convince the unions too. Once the will is there, I hope the resources and facilities can be found.

Certainly the TV companies have an appalling record on training generally and they certainly have enough money to make a contri-

bution I think. How are you actually getting black people now to make programmes?

What I am trying to do, over the first year at least, is to provide work for the existing black film makers. Also, I say to independent producers who I commission, if they come forward with ideas which involve the black community in any way, I am saying, well where are the members of the black community in this proposal? and if there aren't any, and if it is not something that has occurred to the producer, then I would say I think really you should go somewhere else with that particular proposal. Because I am not really interested in a project about, for example, Rastas in Brixton, where there is not a single black person on the production team, and where the Rastas in Brixton are not going to be involved, and the whole thing is going to be from a white perspective. The other thing is basically to find ways of getting people who have done an awful lot of work and have had considerable experience in the ethnic press and various other less mainstream parts of the media, to get them in to television and find some way of training them.

So if there is somebody who has a very strong idea of the programme they would like to make, even if they have not got television experience, are you open to them coming to you with their ideas?

Oh yes. In fact that is happening, but what we then have to do is find a way of matching them with the production skills that they are lacking, and that often takes quite a long time. An example is the Institute of Race Relations. They came to me and said that they wanted to make a series of films on black communities in Britain − smashing idea; good proposals − and Colin Prescod said he wanted to direct them. So he has been going off to various film crews and standing around watching people shooting film, talking to directors, generally trying to learn from productions already going on. He admitted when he came that he didn't feel a hundred per cent confident in directing a film, because he had never directed one, although he had been the assistant director on a number of productions. But he now feels much more confident and he also knows people now that he can call on for advice if anything starts to go wrong.

When somebody switches on to Channel Four to one of your slots, how do you think it will be distinctly different from current BBC or ITV programmes?

Well, they will be covering subjects which have not been covered before. We will be showing things which people haven't seen before. They will be presented by black faces rather than white faces. Wherever possible the production teams will include black people, and in many cases the director or the producer will have been black. Most importantly, our programmes will go out week in, week out, year after year. Multiculturalism will be a continuing presence on Channel 4. That will be distinctly different.

How will the programmes that you make relate to the struggles of the black community – chiefly struggles against white racism in British society.

Given that those are the concerns of the black community, then they will by definition be a part of the programmes that we make. You can't allow in to the media, a whole range of people who have very, very strong views and who want to project their views and their perspective, without those views coming through. The racism in British society is something that every single black person in this country is having to cope with, every single day of their lives, and if they are going to become involved in our programme making then those concerns will almost by definition have to be reflected in the kind of programming we put out. But not all our programmes will be about 'problems'. I am also concerned that we should project positive achievements and contributions that black people have made to Britain as well.

CHANNEL FOUR TELEVISION

Does this herald a brave new world of television?

Many black people I talk to don't have a lot of confidence that Channel Four will be very different, and actually feel that it is part of the white establishment, if you like, that it is the same people who control it, and it will be the same. Do you think that those fears are justified?

I understand those fears, and whatever we do we are never going to satisfy everybody. I think it is a 'no-win' situation, there are always going to be people who feel that we have not done the right thing, but the structure of Channel Four is very different from the structure of other broadcasting systems. There is no question that independent producers who are commissioned by Channel Four have editorial control of the product they are making. They work closely with a Commissioning Editor, who takes a very active and interested role in what they are doing, but that Commissioning Editor is not the person that is making the decisions of what goes into the programme and what doesn't go into it, and how the programme is going to be structured, etc. It is not part of Channel Four's philosophy to do that. The aim is that independent producers are given the freedom to express themselves in the way that they want to do it within the IBA guidelines and the laws of the land, of course. So I think there is very much more chance at Channel Four for black people to make the programmes they want to make and say the things they want to say, than there is at the other channels.

I seem to remember reading somewhere that there is a station in the States that lost its broadcasting franchise because of its coverage of black people — have you heard about it? It seems to me that when the TV companies' franchise are renewed, their record should be something that is actively looked at in terms of the content and their employment policies.

One of the successful ITV companies, in their franchise application made a very strong submission that they were going to be an equal opportunities employer, and in fact have hired a woman engineer, a 100% step forward on last year. There are now two women engineers in ITV. I think it is very important that all of us should be accountable in the area of equal opportunities.

It does seem to me that the women's lobby is much stronger in television.

Well, there are more women working in television, whereas blacks are about five years behind. But I do think that Channel Four offers an opportunity to start to change that, and I am sure that what we do will have a knock-on effect. The one thing that my heart sinks at, is that 5 years ago I wrote a paper for the Edinburgh TV Festival ('In 1968 a black family moved into No. 11 Coronation Street — where are they?') There is a campaign going on at the moment in Sri Lanka to get rid of *Mind Your Language,* and I was rung up by somebody, apparently from the Campaign Against Racism in the Media, Sri Lanka branch. They had heard that I had once written this paper, and they asked me to send them a copy. I read it again before I sent it off to them, and the most depressing thing seems to be the fact that absolutely nothing has changed in those 5 years. If anything everything has got marginally worse.

How do you see things changing in mainstream television?

Well, it is very difficult to know, but it seems to me that unless there are more black people in positions of power, nothing very much will change. One of the problems and the most crucial thing, is that it becomes dependent on a particular individual, and when that individual goes, then you often take ten steps backwards. If it is not somehow more institutionalised, then it is very easy when that particular person leaves for the whole thing to collapse. And I have certainly seen that happen in particular pockets as far as women are concerned. I would like to find a way of somehow creating a structure which is not dependent on the particular views and beliefs and commitments of individuals.

So what does this mean changing exactly?

Well, I think it means having very simple things like, a written policy and somebody who is specifically responsible within the companies for ensuring that this written policy of Equal Opportunities is actually carried out, and monitors it, and ensures that it stays there as a permanent policy. Thames Television have done this quite successfully for women.

Do you think that there should be any changes in the way that the governing bodies of the BBC and ITV are set up? Are you satisfied that they are doing their job properly?

No. I think there should be more black governors at the BBC, and there should be more black people at the IBA both among the officers and members. I am sure if you just got a few black representatives inside the IBA, the whole thing would change in almost no time at all.

You mean that there are no black people at all on the IBA?

There is one black woman member of the Authority, Yvonne Connolly, who has very recently been appointed. I also think there should be at least one black person on the board at Channel Four. The IBA appoints the board of Channel Four so they should be the people who are asked why there isn't. I do feel somehow that the problem has now been identified, it is time to actually start to find ways of doing something about it. Just to go on saying what the problem is and articulating the problem is not going to get anybody anywhere, I mean we really have to focus our energy, our resources and our time.

I think one of the difficulties is that people feel very powerless in the face of media institutions, it is not very clear how you can actually influence what comes out of the box in the corner.

I know, and that actually is entirely the media's fault. It builds up this huge kind of mystique about it all. I mean there is no mystique about making television programmes, there really isn't. It is not beyond the bounds of any perfectly normal reasonably intelligent human being.

Scapegoats of the '30s and '80s

George Jerrom

Take two headlines: 'Aliens pouring into Britain' and 'Smuggling of exiles alarms Britain'. Both have a familiar ring. The first is from the *Daily Mail* in 1938. The second from the *Daily Mirror* in the same year. The headlines referred to Jewish people. They could have been written in recent years in relation to Kenya Asians, Indians, Pakistanis, or refugees from the fascist junta in Chile. Some quotations from the British press in the period 1936-38 plainly show its ideological commitment to capitalism, and its need therefore to direct workers' energies and antagonisms against their own kind rather than the class enemy.

On June 19 1938 the *Sunday Express* carried the following piece of inspired journalism, containing all the pseudo-liberalism and 'fair play' attitude often prevalent in today's journalistic exercises against blacks: 'In Britain half a million Jews find their homes. They are never persecuted and indeed in many respects the Jews are given favoured treatment here. But just now there is a big influx of foreign Jews into Britain. They are over-running the country. They are trying to enter the medical profession in great numbers ... Intolerance is loathed and hated by *almost* everyone in this country... We shall be able to continue to treat well those Jews who have made their homes among us, many of them for generations.' For Jews read blacks, changing the job classifications.

Kingsley Martin in his auto-biography tells us that *The Times* censored all anti-Nazi despatches and that Norman Ebbutt, a respected journalist, lost his job because of his honesty. Louis Heron confirms these learnings in his autobiography. Rothermere commissioned feature writer Ward Price to produce in the *Daily Mail* on September 21 1936 a piece which said in relation to Hitler: 'All Western Europe might soon be clamouring for such a champion.'

* *George Jerrom is a national officer in the National Graphical Association, and was previously NGA Father of the Chapel of the* Daily Mail. *Reprinted from* Free Press, *magazine of The Campaign for Press and Broadcasting Freedom.*

Not to be outdone, Winston Churchill wrote in the *Daily Telegraph* on June 23 1938: 'Without the championship of armed Germany, Sudeten wrongs might never have been redressed.' That was before Churchill recognised Hitler and his creed to be a greater threat to world imperialism than Bolshevism.

The heirs of the Nazis and their ideology are still with us. The same monopoly ownership, now as then, gives blatant and open support to policies and personalities that preach racism, bigotry, intolerance, anti-trade unionism, and anti-socialism. Nothing has changed in the desires and aspirations of these pillars of the establishment and their supporters. But something has changed with the British trade and labour movement. We are stronger! We have the lessons of the past. We are breaking down the ideological-isms that have for too long divided us. We can see major moves to the left on the national executive of the Labour Party and within parliament. The TUC has called major demonstrations against racism, urging the movement to take to the streets to fight racism.

This is still not enough. The lesson of history is that anything that divides; anything that attempts to place worker against worker is anti-trade union and by definition pro-employer. Therefore we should be prepared to act under the rules of our unions against those who preach a doctrine of racism and division. All unions have such disciplinary rules for the protection of the union and its members. Journalists should be more aggressive in the application of the NUJ's code of conduct, and they should recruit the assistance of the production unions in applying industrial pressure at the point of production. The joint NUJ-NGA statement on race reporting (see Appendix) is a sound base. It will not be an easy task, but any failure on our part to face up to the challenge and win will mean a Britain of the right instead of the prospect of socialism.

The drug of racism is easily assimilated. It becomes the excuse for all the political, social, and industrial ills of society. Blame people of a different religion was the option in the '30s. Now the easy answer is to blame people of a different colour. We must not simply say in humanistic fashion that prejudice is wrong. We have to constantly pose the answers and alternatives to the problems created by the system represented by today's Thatcherism – the problems are the daily breeding ground of racism.

Step-by-step guide to fighting racism in the media

Carl Gardner

OK, so you've just read a racist story or item in your local news-paper, or on the radio. What do you do? The following practical guide takes you through the various stages of complaining and hopefully winning some form of redress. Most of these methods are equally applicable to the national media, but except for those living in London or close to the studios of the major regional commercial TV companies, they are rather more difficult to put into practice. It ought to be remembered, too, that TV currently has no mechanism for granting the 'right of reply', though the new Channel Four intends to carry weekly 'alternative' news programmes for those who feel that they have been ignored or misrepresented in the mainstream media.

1. FIRST STEPS

A letter to the editor, for publication in the offending newspaper. Send a copy to the National Union of Journalists (NUJ) Father or Mother of the Chapel (FoC/MoC) at the newspaper, with a copy to the NUJ Race Relations Working Party (see addresses).

If possible write as a member or representative of an organis-ation or if there's time try to get the support of a black or Asian group, anti-racist organisation, Trades Council or Community Relations Council (CRC), as co-signatories.

Disadvantages:
It can be cut or left out at the editor's discretion; it almost certainly won't get the prominence of the offending article; and it may well be 'balanced' by racist letters published alongside it. Readers' letters in newspapers are the commonest way of defusing controversial issues.

TRADE UNIONIST ACTION
In 1979, the editor of the Hornsey Journal wrote a front-page article attacking low-pay strikes. He accused council workers in Haringay of organising a 'carefully orchestrated exercise in trade-union power'. Angry trade unionists contacted the NUJ chapel at the paper, told them they were going to demonstrate outside the newspaper's offices and asked for the journalists' support in demanding the right of reply. They won. The next issue carried both a statement from the strikers and a letter from the journalists dissociating themselves from the editor's article.

GAYS HIT BACK
On June 30, 1979, 10,000 gay men and women took part in a 'Gay Pride' demonstration through London. The following Monday the Guardian carried a report by Peter Cole which treated the demo as a trivial joke − the paper's offices were occupied by a group of gay men and women, who demanded the right of reply. A week later the Guardian carried an extensive article by a group of gays, plus a wide selection of critical correspondence − the editor was anxious to reassure his readers that this response was 'not because of noisy demonstrations'.

2. THE PRESS COUNCIL?

If the issue is of sufficient importance, you may be tempted to go to the Press Council. This is a body set up by government in 1953 supposedly to watch over and 'safeguard' journalistic standards and the readers' interests. It's a toothless watchdog − for example of the 428 complaints submitted to it in 1976, it adjudicated in the complainant's favour in 43 of them. It takes months to deliberate and pass judgement; its decisions have no legal status and newspapers are free to ignore them if they want. Where Press Council decisions against a newspaper are published, they generally get very little prominence. At its 1980 conference the NUJ itself took the decision to dissociate itself from the Council and refused to further co-operate with it − while at the same time seeking to help form a more effective body for press monitoring. Recommendation: Forget it!

3. SOUNDING OUT THE UNIONS

Request a meeting with the NUJ F/MoC of the newspaper or radio-station, or the whole chapel (workplace branch), to bring home your dissatisfaction and to discover the union's attitude to race coverage. Do the problems stem from the staff themselves or 'interference' by the editor (who may or may not be in the union)? Are the NUJ members happy about the paper's coverage of race?

FEMINISTS SHOW THE WAY
In February 1978 the London Evening News *published a story under the headline 'Dr. Strangelove' which attacked the right of lesbians to receive artificial insemination and to conceive and bring up their own children. A group of about 20 to 30 feminists immediately occupied the editorial offices of the newspaper and demanded to see the editor. Before they left he had to promise them the 'right of reply' — three days later they were given a fairly prominent column in the paper to put their views.*

Would they be prepared to take any sort of action on behalf of complainants? Do they know and understand NUJ policy on race-reporting?

Always attend such meetings in a body of at least two or three, preferably drawn from a representative range of groups. You should contact local black and ethnic groups, anti-racist organisations, sympathetic CRCs, Trades Councils, Labour Party branches and others for support.

Contact the Campaign for Press and Broadcasting Freedom (CPBF) to see if they have a local group willing to help (see addresses).

4. SPREADING THE NET

It might also be useful at this time to contact the other unions in the press or station, via their F/MoCs or officials, to discover their attitude – NGA and SOGAT 82 in the print. ABAS in BBC local radio and TV, ACTT in commercial television. It might be appropriate to send your complaint to the regional branch of the NUJ, under which workplace chapels are organised, if you have no response at the local level. Ask for the issue to be discussed at their monthly meeting and offer to send a speaker. Branch secretaries addresses can be obtained from the NUJ Head Office (see addresses).

MEETING THE TOTTENHAM WEEKLY HERALD
Throughout 1975-6 North London's Tottenham Weekly Herald *had run a series of racist stories, with headlines like 'WHAT ABOUT US WHITES, ASKS ANGRY COUNCILLOR' and 'BLACK GIRLS' BRUTAL ATTACK ON HOME HELP', as well as giving space to racist letters in its columns. Members of the NUJ Race Relations Sub-Committee had already paid a visit to the chapel to discuss their race coverage. CARM approached a local Community Relations officer and suggested he call a meeting with the paper's journalists. In August 1976 half a dozen Herald staffers met thirty representatives of black organisations, the Labour Party and the Trades Council, the North London NUJ branch and CARM, at a public meeting. It was an often stormy confrontation. From that meeting an anti-racist committee was formed locally which decided to make the Herald a focus for its activity. Some weeks later the committee picketed the paper, distributing leaflets to passers-by and journalists going in and out. These actions and the decision of the North London branch of the NUJ to bring complaints against Herald staff under the Union Code of Conduct were undoubtedly successful in bringing about a change in the paper's race policy. Blatant anti-black propaganda became increasingly rare.*

IRELAND AND THE RIGHT OF REPLY
In May 1981 the Western Mail *in Cardiff published an editorial about the death of hunger-striker/MP Bobby Sands, under the headlines 'SANDS NO MARTYR, JUST A CRIMINAL'. A picket of its offices by the Cardiff Irish Solidarity Committee protesting over the piece brought the editor to the door and resulted in the publication of the committee's press statement, together with a picture and report of the picket.*

---

5. GOING PUBLIC

Should none of this achieve the desired result – and you believe the particular incident or persistent racist coverage is sufficiently important – it's time to go public. With the support of other groups, seek to organise a public meeting in the area, to discuss the issue of local race coverage in the media. Invite the editor and journalists of the paper or station to debate with you in public. Issue a press statement to the other local media, plus all potentially interested groups or individuals (the local council, political parties etc.)

6. DIRECT ACTION

From the public meeting, if necessary, you could go on to organise more direct forms of action against the offending media, such as a picket or even an occupation of the newspaper offices, to demand the right of reply. In either case print a leaflet for distribution to passers-by, staff entering the building, customers at local news-agents, explaining your case.

7. THE RIGHT OF REPLY

Clause 4 of the NUJ Code of Conduct (see Appendix) states that journalists should 'afford the right of reply to persons criticised when the issue is of sufficient importance'. The demand for 'the right of reply' has recently been taken up in a big way by several unions, and particularly the CPBF, and is seen as a major interim step towards a freer press. As a demand it can be clearly seen as *extending* the range of views in the media, not restricting them. Perhaps equally importantly the 'right of reply' demand is one that can unite readers and workers in the industry around particular cases of misrepresentation – and can encourage trade unionists to consider the content of the press and their own role in producing it. For a longer discussion of this issue, see Aidan White's article in this volume.

8. AN NUJ COMPLAINT

Clause 10 of the NUJ Code of Conduct states that 'journalists should not originate material which encourages discrimination on grounds of race, colour, creed, gender or sexual orientation'. This is supposed to be binding on all members of the union − *individual* members offending against this code can have a formal complaint taken out against them under rule by any other member of the union, which may lead to disciplinary action. Non-NUJ members have to find a sympathetic NUJ member to put in a complaint on their behalf − this will be first considered by the complainant's branch. If it's felt there's a case to answer, it will then be passed on to the National Office for adjudication. While the union's Code of Conduct has yet to gain real teeth, complaints stimulate discussion and are to be encouraged. For further details of the procedure and difficulties involved, see Phil Cohen's article on the NUJ and race.

9. ONGOING ACTION

Biased, misrepresentative reporting is not confined to the issue of race − trade unionists, women, gays and political organisations outside the mainstream all suffer at the hands of the media. You could form a regular, permanent monitoring group under one umbrella in your locality to survey the national and local media and to suggest and initiate appropriate forms of action.

Affiliate to the national Campaign for Press and Broadcasting Freedom (see addresses) − a broad left body working to open up the media to greater accountability, access and diversification, and for the general principle of the 'right of reply' for all those maligned in the press and broadcasting.

THE FRONT ON RADIO
In 1976 the management of Radio Trent agreed to drop a phone-in programme with a local National Front leader when anti-fascists made clear that a major demonstration would be held outside if the station went ahead.

MONITORING THE LOCAL MEDIA
The Harrow Observer *is a consistently Tory newspaper. Sick of its bias, the local Trades Council, National Abortion Campaign, women's group, anti-racist committee, Campaign for Homosexual Equality and other organisations came together in May 1980 to pool their experience and to set up a monitoring group to compile a dossier on the* Observer's *reporting, for submission to the paper's NUJ chapel.*

APPENDIX 1

NUJ code of conduct

1. A journalist has a duty to maintain the highest professional and ethical standards.
2. A journalist shall at all times defend the principle of the freedom of the press and other media in relation to the collection of information and the expression of comment and criticism. He/she shall strive to eliminate distortion, news suppression and censorship.
3. A journalist shall strive to ensure that the information he/she disseminates is fair and accurate, avoid the expression of comment and conjecture as established fact and falsification by distortion, selection or misrepresentation.
4. A journalist shall rectify promptly any harmful inaccuracies, ensure the correction and apologies receive due prominence and afford the right of reply to persons criticised when the issue is of sufficient importance.
5. A journalist shall obtain information, photographs and illustrations only by straightforward means. The use of other means can be justified only by over-riding considerations of the public interest. The journalist is entitled to exercise a personal conscientious objection to the use of such means.
6. Subject to justification by over-riding considerations of public interest, a journalist shall do nothing which entails intrusion into private grief and distress.
7. A journalist shall protect confidential sources of information.
8. A journalist shall not accept bribes nor shall he/she allow other inducements to influence the performances of his/her professional duties.
9. A journalist shall not lend himself/herself to the distortion or suppression of the truth because of advertising or other considerations.
10. A journalist shall not originate material which encourages discrimination on grounds of race, colour, creed, gender or sexual orientation.
11. A journalist shall not take private advantage of information gained in the course of his/her duties, before the information is public knowledge.

NUJ race relations guidelines

The National Union of Journalists has ratified guidelines for all its members to follow when dealing with race relations subjects. If YOU are a member, these are YOUR guidelines:
— Only mention someone's race or nationality if strictly relevant.
— Resist the temptation to sensationalise issues which could harm race relations
— Press for equal opportunities for employment of black staff, particularly in areas of extensive minority group settlement
— Seek to achieve wider and better coverage of black affairs: social, political, cultural
— Investigate the treatment of blacks in education, employment and housing and the activities of racialist organisations

These guidelines relate to Clause 10 of the revised code of conduct, which was approved at the 1975 Annual Delegates Meeting in Cardiff. This Clause enjoins journalists not to 'originate material which encourages discrimination on grounds of race, colour, creed, gender or sexual orientation'.

The 1977 Annual Delegates Meeting decided to 'instruct every branch to set up a watch-dog committee to monitor racial stories and report any instance of a breach of the NUJ Code of Conduct to the Race Relations Working Party'.

APPENDIX 3

Guidelines on reporting racist organisations

The following guidelines (with one or two additions) were formulated by the London North Branch of the NUJ in 1977. To date they represent the fullest elaboration of practical guidelines for dealing with racist organisations like the National Front in the media − and go far beyond the general approach adopted by the NUJ nationally, in its official publications.

Recommendations

1. Where stories about racist organisations are being published, write critically of their anti-social stance and actively seek rebutting comments from their opponents. Check the accuracy of all reports.
2. Seek to publish 'feature' articles criticising the racist policies of organisations like the National Front and National 'Party' and provide readers with a detailed case arguing against their point of view.
3. Investigate the activities of racist organisations and expose behaviour/ policies that are to their disadvantage.
4. Be aware of increasingly sophisticated propaganda tactics. Not all racists exploit thuggery and military-style motorcades.
5. If asked to cover NF or NP meetings stick strictly to the NUJ's code of conduct. Feel free to act according to conscience either by refusing to attend or in deliberately writing a report that is either extremely brief or highly critical. Obtain the protection of your chapel if there is any danger of your editors trying to take disciplinary action or 'doctoring' your copy so that the stand you have taken is nullified.
6. Draw the attention of the public to the fascist aspects of the policies of these organisations. Many people are instinctively against fascism, yet fail to realise it is manifest in the basic policies of the NF and NP.
7. Actively support and *report* the activities of anti-racist organisations. Do not rely on them feeding stories to you − go out to them!
8. Enthusiastically take up issues like immigration and deportation.
9. Don't 'respectabalise' racist organisations and accord them the status of a bona-fide political party by straightforwardly reporting their statements.
10. Don't shirk from confronting your management, even if it means taking industrial action, when it means establishing a constructive policy to race reporting.
11. Do not allow the letters column or 'phone-in' programmes to be used to spread racial hatred.

APPENDIX 4

NUJ – NGA Agreement on race

The NGA and the NUJ believe that the development of racist attitudes and the growth of the fascist parties pose a threat to democracy, the right of trade union organisations, a free press and the development of social harmony and well-being.

The NGA and the NUJ believe that members of their unions cannot avoid a measure of responsibility in fighting the evil of racism as expressed through the mass media.

The NGA and the NUJ reaffirm their total opposition to censorship but equally reaffirm their belief that press freedom must be conditioned by responsibility and an acknowledgement by all media workers of the need not to allow press freedom to be abused to slander a section of the community or to promote the evil of racism.

The NGA and the NUJ believe that the methods and lies of the racists should be publicly and vigorously exposed.

The NGA and the NUJ believe that newspapers and magazines should not originate material which encourages discrimination on grounds of race or colour as expressed in the NUJ's Rule Book and Code of Conduct.

The NGA and the NUJ recognise the right of members to withhold their labour on grounds of conscience because employers are providing a platform for racist propaganda.

The NGA and the NUJ believe that editors should ensure that coverage of race stories should be placed in a balanced context.

The NGA and the NUJ will continue to monitor the development of media coverage in this area and give mutual support to members of each union seeking to enforce the aims outlined in this joint statement.

APPENDIX 5

ACTT code on race

1. ACTT members should not originate material which encourages discrimination or incites hatred on the grounds of race, colour, creed or national origin.
2. Members working in news and current affairs should ensure that coverage of race relations is fair and accurate; and particularly:
   a) That a person's race, colour, creed or national origin should be mentioned only when strictly relevant to the story;
   b) That, when racialist allegations are made or racialist views are expressed, black and/or anti-racialist organisations should be granted automatic and contemporaneous right of reply;
   c) That issues which could harm race relations are not sensationalised;
   d) That the sympathetic presentation of racialist ideas should be discouraged.
3. In the fields of Drama and Light Entertainment, members should seek to portray blacks and other ethnic minorities as ordinary members of the community, and avoid the exclusive presentation of blacks and ethnic minorities in the context of race or immigration, and should seek to avoid the portrayal of racial and ethnic minorities in a disparaging manner based upon their race or ethnic origin.
4. Members should seek to achieve a wider coverage of black and other ethnic minority affairs: social, political and cultural.
5. Members should press for equal employment opportunities for all people regardless of their race, colour, creed or national origin and should insist that the TUC's Equal Opportunities Clause is included in all agreements with employing bodies.

Addresses

NUJ Head Office and NUJ Race Relations Sub-Committee,
  314 Gray's Inn Road, London WC1 (01-278 7916)
BBC TV Centre, Wood Lane, London W12 (01-743 8000)
BBC (Radio), Broadcasting House, London W1A 1AA (01-580 4468)
ACTT, 2 Soho Square, London W1 (01-437 8506)
Association of Broadcasting Staffs, 16 Goodge Street, London W1
  (01-637 1261)
NGA, 63-67 Bromham Road, Bedford, Beds. MK40 2AG (0234 51521)
SOGAT 82, 274-288 London Road, Hadleigh, Essex. SS7 2DE
  (0702 553131)
NATSOPA, 13-16 Borough Road, London SE1 0AL
Independent Broadcasting Authority, 17 Brompton Road, London SW3
  (01-584 7011)
Advertising Standards Authority, Brook House, Torrington Place,
  London WC1 (01-580 5555)
Campaign Against Racism in the Media, PO Box 50, London N1
Campaign for Press and Broadcasting Freedom, 274-288 London Road,
  Hadleigh, Essex, SS7 5DE (0702 553131 and 01-437 2795)
Black Media Workers' Association, 180b Holland Road, London W14
  (01-602 7694)

:d bibliography

RACE AND THE MEDIA

Campaign Against Racism in the Media (CARM): *In Black and White* (London, 1977) – out of print.

Critcher, Parker and Sondhi: 'Race in the Provincial Press' in *Ethnicity and the Media* (UNESCO Press, 1977)

John Downing: *The Media Machine* (Pluto Press, 1980) – Chaps 3, 4.

P. Evans: *Publish and Be Damned?* (Runnymede Trust, 1976)

Hartman & Husband: *Racism in the Mass Media* (Davis Poynter, 1974)

Charles Husband (ed.): *White Media and Black Britain* (Arrow Books, 1975)

Charles Husband: 'News Media, Language and Race Relations: A Case Study in Identity Maintenance' in *Language, Ethnicity and Intergroup Behaviour* (ed. H. Giles) (Academic Press, 1979)

Francesca Klug: *Racist Attacks* (Runnymede Trust, 1982)

Denis MacShane: *Black & Front: Journalists and Race Reporting* (NUJ, 1978)

National Association of Multiracial Education: *Multiracial Education* Vol 9, No 1. Special double issue on Race and the Media, including articles on blacks in films, black employment in the media and the media and the Third World.

Lord Scarman: *The Brixton Disorders 10-12 April, 1981* (HMSO, 1981)

John Thackara: 'The Mass Media and Racism' in *Media, Politics and Culture* (ed. C. Gardner) (Macmillan, 1979)

Tracey and Troyna: 'What Could the BBC Do About the NF?' in *Broadcast* (April 30, 1979)

Barry Troyna: *Public Awareness and the Media: A Study of Reporting on Race* (CRE Publication, 1981)

Barry Troyna: 'Images of Race and Racist Images in the British News Media' in *Mass Media and Mass Communications* (ed. J.D. Halloran) (Leicester University Press, 1981)

Barry Troyna: 'Reporting the National Front: British Values Observed' in *Race in Britain: Continuity and Change* (ed. C. Husband) (Open University/Hutchinson, 1981)

GENERAL

John Fiske and John Hartley: *Reading Television* (Methuen, 1978)

James Curran and Jean Seaton: *Power Without Responsibility: The Press and Broadcasting in Britain* (Fontana, 1981)

Carl Gardner (ed.): *Media, Politics and Culture: A Socialist View* (Macmillan, 1979)

Stuart Hood: *On Television* (Pluto, 1980)

John Downing: *The Media Machine* (Pluto, 1980)

Stuart Hall, C. Critcher et al: *Policing the Crisis* (Macmillan, 1978)

Glasgow University Media Group: *Really Bad News* (Writers & Readers, 1982)

Denis MacShane: *Using the Media* (Pluto, 1979)

Free Press, bi-monthly bulletin of the Campaign for Press and Broadcasting Freedom

It Ain't Half Racist, Mum, 30-minute film/video. See article 'It Ain't Half a Hot Potato, Mum' for hire details.

Comedia Publishing Group